Active Learning
in the
MATHEMATICS
CLASSROOM
Grades 5-8
Second Edition

Active Learning
in the
MATHEMATICS CLASSROOM
Grades 5-8

Second Edition of
Multiple Intelligences
in the Mathematics Classroom

HOPE MARTIN

CORWIN PRESS
A SAGE Publications Company
Thousand Oaks, CA 91320

For information:

Corwin Press
A Sage Publications Company
2455 Teller Road
Thousand Oaks, California 91320
www.corwinpress.com

SAGE Publications Ltd.
1 Oliver's Yard
55 City Road
London EC1Y 1SP
United Kingdom

SAGE Publications India Pvt. Ltd.
B 1/I 1 Mohan Cooperative
     Industrial Area
Mathura Road, New Delhi
India 110 044

SAGE Publications Asia-Pacific Pvt Ltd
33 Pekin Street #02-01
Far East Square
Singapore   048763

Printed in the United States of America.

Library of Congress Cataloging-in-Publication Data

Martin, Hope.
Active learning in the mathematics classroom, grades 5-8 / Hope Martin. -- 2nd ed.
     p. cm.
Includes bibliographical references.
ISBN-13: 978–1–4129–4977–4 (cloth)
ISBN-13: 978–1–4129–4978–1 (pbk.)
   1. Mathematics—Study and teaching (Elementary) 2. Active learning. I. Title.
QA135.5.M3662 2007
372.7'044—dc22

2006034106

This book is printed on acid-free paper.

07   08   09   10   11   10   9   8   7   6   5   4   3   2   1

Acquisitions Editor:	Cathy Hernandez
Editorial Assistants:	Charline Wu & Megan Bedell
Production Editor:	Jenn Reese
Copy Editor:	Marilyn Power Scott
Typesetter:	C&M Digitals (P) Ltd.
Proofreader:	Joyce Li
Cover Designer:	Michael Dubowe
Graphic Designer:	Karine Hovsepian
Illustrator:	Robert Griesen

Contents

Preface   **vii**
    How the Chapters Are Organized

Acknowldgments   **xiii**

About the Author   **xv**

Alignment With NCTM Standards   **xvi**

**1. Investigations: Estimation, Large Numbers,
   and Numeration**   **1**
    $1,000,000 Long   6
    How Many Strides to Walk Around the Earth?   9
    Rectangles and Factors   13
    Venn Diagrams: LCM and GCF   16
    Dessert for a Crowd   20
    5 × 5 Puzzle Cents   24
    Chocolate Chip Cookies   28
    Music and Fractions   31
    Mathematical Palindromes   36

2. Active Algebra   **43**
    Patterns, Patterns, Patterns   47
    Algebra Jokes   54
    The M&M's Mystery   59
    Algebra Match   63
    Inequality Number Line Match   67
    Mind Reading or Algebra?   71

3. Geometry: Our Mathematical Window to the World   **77**
    Folding a Tangram   82
    Making a Tangram Quilt   87
    Pentominoes   92
    Open-Top Boxes   97
    Explorations With Cereal Boxes   100
    The Painted Cube   104
    Cubes That Grow   107

4. The Measure of Mathematics   **111**
    Just How Big Is the Statue of Liberty?   116
    Gummi Worms   121
    What Happened 1,000,000 Seconds Ago?   125

How Long Would It Take to Walk to China—
  Through the Center of the Earth?   128
Height Versus Shoe Length   131
EggsCetera   135

5. Data Collection and Probability   **141**
Super Survey   146
What Is Your Favorite Subject?   151
Stars of the NBA   157
Dice and Probability   166
Is This Game Fair?   173
Dinosaurs and Probability   180

**Resource: Interactive Web Sites to Make
Math–Technology Connections**   **185**

References   **187**

Preface

Education is not the filling of a pail, but the lighting of a fire.

—William Butler Yeats

An old Chinese proverb says, "I hear, and I forget; I see, and I remember; I do, and I understand." Consider trying to learn to dance by reading a book and memorizing the steps or learning to drive a car by reading the manual . . . we learn when we are actively involved in the learning process and use a variety of learning modalities. Not all students have the same talents, learn the same way, or have the same interests and abilities. But all students must have access to high-quality mathematics instruction.

The National Research Council (1989) stated, "Research on learning shows that most students cannot learn mathematics effectively by only listening and imitating; yet most teachers teach mathematics this way. Most teachers teach as they were taught, not as they were taught to teach" (p. 6).

The Foundation Coalition (n.d.) asks "Why don't we teach the way students learn?" Their *Cone of Learning* compares how much we remember with how it is taught. They maintain that we remember 10% of what we read, 20% of what we hear, 50% of what we both see and hear, but 90% of what we do—what we are actively involved in. By participating in a real experience or simulation, students are involved and motivated, and the learning curve rises dramatically. Ahmed (1987), in *Better Mathematics*, agrees: "Mathematics can be effectively learned only by involving pupils in experimenting, questioning, reflecting, discovering, inventing, and discussing" (p. 24).

Van de Walle (2006) describes the current teaching of mathematics in the following way: "Traditional teaching, still the predominant instructional pattern, typically begins with an explanation of whatever idea is on the current page of the text, followed by showing children how to do the assigned exercises. . . . The focus of the lesson is primarily on getting answers" (p. 12). The result of this style of instruction is that a large number of today's students are not prepared for the realities of living in the 21st century.

The National Council of Teachers of Mathematics (NCTM; 2000) in *Principles and Standards for School Mathematics*, says, "In this changing world, those who understand and do mathematics will have significantly enhanced opportunities and options for shaping their future. A lack of mathematical competence keeps those doors closed." The Council has called for "a common foundation of mathematics to be learned by all students" (p. 5). In this document, the NCTM has divided 10 standards into two groups: the *Content Standards* and the *Process Standards.* The five Content Standards—number and operations, algebra, geometry, measurement, and data analysis and probability—clearly describe the content that students should learn. The five Process Standards—problem solving, reasoning and proof, communication, connections, and representation—illustrate what students should be doing to acquire and use the content knowledge. "This set of ten Standards does not neatly separate the school mathematics curriculum into nonintersecting subsets. . . . Process can be learned within the Content Standards and content can be learned within the Process Standards. Rich connections and intersections abound" (pp. 30–31).

The investigations in *Active Learning in the Mathematics Classroom* have been designed to keep students in Grades 5 through 8 *actively involved in the learning of mathematics.* I concur that "mathematics is not a spectator sport," and this maxim has been the guiding principle behind the structure of this book. Chapters have been organized around the five Content Standards, but as stated above, the strands cannot be separated into nonintersecting subsets, and so all of the activities connect many mathematics skills and concepts. The way each activity ties to the standards is shown in Table P.1, Alignment With NCTM Standards, which immediately precedes Chapter 1.

This second edition has undergone some significant changes:

- The material has been updated and now includes Web sites that can be used as enrichment and bring technology into the mathematics classroom.
- A new chapter, "Active Algebra," has been added to reflect the changes in the middle school mathematics curriculum.
- There are 15 new activities.
- The outline and organization of the chapters have been altered to better reflect the recommendations of the NCTM (2000) in the *Principles and Standards for School Mathematics* and current research on active learning.

These are brief descriptions of the chapters included in the second edition:

Chapter 1, "Investigations: Estimation, Large Numbers, and Numeration," gives students the opportunity to collect data using very large numbers, use unique ways to revisit number theory, and explore real-world applications or recipes and music to reinforce their understanding of fractions.

Chapter 2, "Active Algebra," is a new addition to the book. Ten years ago it was not common for middle school students to be studying algebra. But in today's classrooms, many students of this age are introduced to or actively involved in the study of this strand of mathematics. For this reason, motivating activities have been added to meet these needs. Manipulatives are used to give students a tactile experience with patterns; algebra jokes provide a self-correcting way to help students solve linear equations and solve geometric problems; data collection and the use of variables are merged in a tasty activity; and verbal, algebraic, and graphic representations are combined to help students make important connections.

Chapter 3, "Geometry: Our Mathematical Window to the World," includes a variety of activities to help students progress through van Hiele's levels of geometric learning (as cited in Fuys, Geddes, & Tischler, 1988). Dina van

Table P.2   van Hiele's First Three Levels

Level	Name	How Might the Child Describe a Parallelogram?
0	Visual level/Visualization	It looks like a slanted rectangle.
1	Descriptive level/Analysis	It has parallel sides.
2	Informal deductive level/ Reasoning	It is a quadrilateral whose opposite sides are parallel and equal.

Hiele-Geldof and Pierre van Hiele hypothesized five levels of geometric thinking. They believed that only when children achieved a firm understanding of geometric concepts at a lower level were they able to move on to a higher level. While the van Hieles put forward five levels, only three of these strongly relate to students at the middle school level. These are shown in Table P.2.

If a child is still at Level 0, "It looks like it, therefore it is," the van Hieles contend that they cannot move on to Level 1, the descriptive level—a higher level of understanding. For this reason, hands-on activities, such as paper folding, measuring, and building, help students discover empirically the properties or rules of a class of both two-dimensional and three-dimensional shapes.

Chapter 4, "The Measure of Mathematics," employs current research recommendations by getting students actively involved in tasks that use both metric and customary units, using scale factors and selecting appropriate units of measure. Students are encouraged to measure and then use ratio, proportion, and scale drawing to reproduce the Statue of Liberty, make use of the distance formula to walk through the center of the Earth, experiment with scatterplots as a way to compare two measurements, and make real-world consumer connections.

Chapter 5, "Data Collection and Probability," demonstrates the data collection process by taking students through the four steps: collection, organization, analysis, and graphic representation. In today's world, we are overwhelmed with a plethora of statistics. Using data supplied by the National Basketball Association (NBA), students are encouraged to recognize the value of graphic representations to make sense of a large amount of data. The three activities related to probability ask students to discover possible outcomes, determine the "fairness" of a game based upon odds, and make predictions based upon their experimental results.

HOW THE CHAPTERS ARE ORGANIZED

Brief Introduction: At the beginning of each chapter, there is a brief description of the activities and the mathematical concepts contained in the chapter.

Teacher's Pages: There are several pages of planning information for each activity. These pages contain the following:

1. *Math Topics:* This is a listing of the mathematics skills and concepts that are contained in this lesson. Because of the richness of the activities, there will always be more than one skill listed in this area.

2. *Active Learning:* This section lists what the students will do. It may also recommend a flexible grouping arrangement. A careful analysis of these concepts will help define the components for authentic assessment.

3. *Materials:* This section lists the supplies and materials needed for students to begin the activity. For example, if an overhead transparency is needed for follow-up work with students, it will be listed here. If calculators are listed, they are necessary because of the complexity of the computations. Having these supplies and materials on hand will help make the activity run smoothly and efficiently.

4. *Suggestions for Instruction:* This area has been expanded in this edition. It has been designed to give the teacher an idea of how to begin and of what might happen during the lesson. Most often, this section begins with a question to be posed to the students. For example, "What do you think will happen if . . . ?" "Have you ever considered the possibility that . . . ?" or "How do you think we might attempt to figure that out?" You would never want to say something like, "Don't do it that way" or "You must always do it this way." Instead, serve as a facilitator or guide to the students. I would caution you to follow two very important rules:

- Go with the flow—give your students the opportunity to explore their own solutions. It is amazing the creativity students will use when they can plan and organize in a cooperative group.
- Don't be the sage on the stage—don't feel that you must tell your students "how to do it" or what the answer is. Give them the opportunity to experiment with various strategies and use their multiple intelligences and learning strengths. When you give students a "rule," you are limiting their solution strategies to one right way and may, in fact, be hindering rather than encouraging their learning.

If there are interesting Web sites or references that can be used to enhance the lesson, these will be included in this section as well.

5. *Selected Answers:* When a lesson has a unique answer, it will be found in this section, rather than at the back of the book as in the first edition.

6. *Variation:* This section describes supplementary or extension activities for the lesson. It might extend the activity to a longer project, develop the same concepts using additional activities, or be something that challenges your "better" math students. Use your creativity—add variations and design your own activities using the materials and models.

7. *Writing in Math:* The journal questions provide students an opportunity to express their knowledge using language rather than mathematical symbols and rules. In this edition, it might include a problem similar to the one in the activity and so it can be used as one assessment component. Or it might ask students to describe the procedures they used while solving the problem. Expressing their thoughts in this way gives the teacher a clearer indication of how well they each understood the mathematics embedded in the activity. In this edition, there will usually be two journal questions. These can be used to

differentiate instruction, as one of the questions is usually more difficult than the other.

The Math Investigation: ready-to-use activities follow the teacher's planning pages. The 15 new activities in the second edition include investigations related to algebra, data collection, and measurement. In addition, many of the activities have been revised and updated. Interesting Web sites have been added to provide technology options. All the activities have all been designed to give students the opportunity to become actively involved in learning mathematics by using manipulatives, making connections to real-world applications, or addressing their different learning styles and multiple intelligences.

At the back of the book, there is a Resource section that lists interactive Web sites to make math–technology connections. Following it, the Bibliography consists of a list of references related to curriculum, assessment, and current research. The Web sites listed are those that encourage student's active involvement. Many of these sites can be used to enrich topics other than those presented in this book. Be sure to explore them fully and add them to your activity list.

What we learn to do, we learn by doing.
—Aristotle

Acknowledgments

My thanks to my husband, Arnie, who has supported my endeavors, taken pride in my accomplishments, and been my friend for almost half a century.

Publisher's Acknowledgments

Corwin Press gratefully acknowledges the contributions of the following reviewers:

Patricia Allanson
Seventh-Grade Mathematics Teacher
Deltona Middle School
Deltona, FL

Zoma Barrett
Mathematics, Broadcast Journalism, and Computer Science Teacher
Salem Middle School
Salem, IN

Dawn Brailsford
Mathematics Teacher
Murray Middle School
St. Augustine, FL

Joan Commons
Coordinator of the Elementary Math and Science Institute
University of California–San Diego
San Diego, CA

Jim Dorward
Professor of Elementary Education
Utah State University
Logan, UT

Dewey Gottlieb
Mathematics Resource Teacher
Pearl City High School
Pearl City, HI

xiv   ACTIVE LEARNING IN THE MATHEMATICS CLASSROOM, GRADES 5–8

Vena M. Long
Professor of Mathematics Education
University of Tennessee
Knoxville, TN

Holly Savoie
Third-Grade Teacher
Mimosa Park Elementary School
Luling, LA

P. Mark Taylor
Assistant Professor of Mathematics Education
University of Tennessee
Knoxville, TN

About the Author

 **Hope Martin** is an innovative mathematics teacher with over 40 years of experience. Having worked with children in elementary, middle, and high school, and with teachers in local universities, she is currently a private educational consultant facilitating workshops in the United States, Canada, and Iceland. Her spoon collection confirms her visits to 42 states, two Canadian provinces, and one country that spans both North America and Europe: Iceland is the site of part of the Mid-Atlantic Ridge, where the North American plate is pulling away from the European plate. So Iceland lies both in North America and Europe.

Hope was born and raised in the Bronx, New York, receiving her bachelor's degree from Brooklyn College. She began her teaching career in Skokie, Illinois, and helped design the mathematics program related to the "New Math" that gained popularity during the 1960s. She left the classroom for eight years, raising her children and obtaining her master's degree in Mathematics Education from Northeastern Illinois University.

Returning to teaching in 1973, Hope saw a drastic change in the educational climate. Schools were now teaching a back-to-the-basics curriculum. The math pendulum continues to swing back and forth between innovative and traditional philosophies. However, Hope's personal experiences and knowledge of educational learning theories has convinced her that students learn mathematics more effectively when they are active participants and see its relevance to their own lives. Learning math must be a sense-making experience for effective learning to take place!

Hope lives with her husband, Arnie, in Buffalo Grove, Illinois. Arnie is a musician who helps her with her math songs. She has three grown children, Wendy, Shawn, and Lynne; a daughter-in-law, Jill; and two grandchildren, 9-year-old Joshua and 6-year-old Stephanie. She is thrilled that they all live within three miles of each other.

Alignment With NCTM Standards

Table P.1

EXPLORATION	Number & Operation	Algebra	Geometry	Measurement	Data Analysis & Probability	Problem Solving	Reasoning & Proof	Communication	Connections	Representation
	Content Standards					*Process Standards*				
Investigations: Estimation, Large Numbers, and Numeration										
$1,000,000 Long	•			•		•		•	•	
How Many Strides to Walk Around the Earth?	•			•	•	•		•	•	
Rectangles and Factors	•		•	•		•		•		•
Venn Diagrams: LCM & GCF	•		•			•	•	•	•	•
Dessert for a Crowd	•	•		•		•	•	•	•	
5 × 5 Puzzle Cents	•						•	•	•	
Chocolate Chip Cookies	•			•		•		•	•	
Music and Fractions	•					•		•	•	•
Mathematical Palindromes	•				•	•		•	•	
Active Algebra										
Patterns, Patterns, Patterns	•	•				•	•	•		
Algebra Jokes	•	•	•			•		•		
The M&M's Mystery	•	•				•		•	•	•
Algebra Match	•	•				•	•	•	•	•
Inequality–Number–Line Match	•	•				•	•	•	•	•
Mind Reading or Algebra?	•	•				•	•	•	•	
Geometry: Our Mathematical Window to the World										
Folding a Tangram			•	•				•	•	
Making a Tangram Quilt	•		•	•		•		•	•	
Pentominoes			•	•	•	•		•		
Open-Top Boxes	•	•	•		•	•		•		
Explorations With Cereal Boxes	•	•	•			•		•		
The Painted Cube		•	•		•	•	•	•		
Cubes That Grow	•	•	•		•	•	•	•	•	•

	Content Standards					Process Standards				
EXPLORATION	*Number & Operation*	*Algebra*	*Geometry*	*Measurement*	*Data Analysis & Probability*	*Problem Solving*	*Reasoning & Proof*	*Communication*	*Connections*	*Representation*
The Measure of Mathematics										
Just How Big Is the Statue of Liberty?	•			•	•	•		•	•	•
Gummi Worms	•		•	•	•	•		•	•	•
What Happened 1,000,000 Seconds Ago?	•			•		•		•	•	
How Long Would It Take to Walk to China . . . ?	•			•	•	•		•	•	
Height Versus Shoe Length	•			•	•	•	•	•	•	•
EggsCetera	•	•	•	•	•	•		•	•	
Data Collection & Probability										
Super Survey	•		•	•	•	•		•	•	•
What Is Your Favorite Subject?	•		•	•	•	•		•	•	•
Stars of the NBA	•				•	•		•	•	
Dice and Probability	•				•	•	•	•	•	•
Is This Game Fair?					•	•		•	•	
Dinosaurs and Probability	•				•	•	•	•		

Investigations 1

Estimation, Large Numbers, and Numeration

Investigations 1

Estimation, Large Numbers, and Numeration

Arithmetic is numbers you squeeze from your head to your hand to your pencil to your paper till you get the answer.

—Carl Sandburg, "Arithmetic"

Mathematics can be a powerful tool for students—and us—to make sense of the world around them. Without good estimation skills, we cannot approximate distances, or the number of people in a crowd, or how much our grocery bill will be, looking at a shopping cart full of groceries. Without an adequate understanding of large numbers, we cannot conceive of the enormity of a deficit of $5,000,000,000,000 (five trillion dollars) or the need to change an area code to provide the telephone company with additional telephone numbers. Without a secure understanding of relationships between numbers, we are unable to fully comprehend fractions, decimals, and percentages.

In the middle grades, students "should understand numbers, ways of representing numbers, relationships among numbers, and number systems" (National Council of Teachers of Mathematics [NCTM], 2000, p. 214). In addition, they need to "understand meanings of operations and how they relate to one another . . . and compute fluently and make reasonable estimates" (p. 214). The activities in this chapter will encourage students to do the following:

- Estimate when working with large numbers and distances in real-life problems
- Problem solve strategies to find reasonable answers to motivating problems
- Investigate fractions and decimals in a variety of real-world and problem-solving situations
- Use hands-on activities to make connections between abstract concepts and the concrete models that represent them

What better way to develop good number concepts than through interesting and motivating activities that keep students *actively learning* mathematics!

$1,000,000 LONG

This activity is an open-ended problem that encourages students to explore strategies, work collaboratively, make mathematical connections to social studies, and examine alternative solutions when dealing with large numbers. This activity asks students to use their knowledge of the length of one dollar bill to extrapolate the length of one million of them—the perfect opportunity for an authentic discussion of just how precise is precise?"

HOW MANY STRIDES TO WALK AROUND THE EARTH?

This is another open-ended problem that requires each group to develop its own unique problem-solving strategies when pacing off a very large number of steps. The initial problem necessitates figuring out what a group's *normal* stride is. In the process of solving this problem, students work collaboratively, make mathematical connections to science, and use rounded numbers as they ponder precision and accuracy.

RECTANGLES AND FACTORS

Students use square tiles to discover the relationship between rectangular arrays and prime and composite numbers. When students use manipulative materials and reasoning skills to discover an abstract relationship, the learning is more meaningful and permanent. By associating numbers with their factors in an area model, students acquire a deeper and longer-lasting understanding.

VENN DIAGRAMS: LCM AND GCF

This activity helps students see the mathematical relationship between the greatest common factor (GCF) and least common multiple (LCM). The visual model supplied by the Venn diagram helps students associate abstract number theory with its visual representation and brings it into the "mind's eye" of the student.

DESSERT FOR A CROWD

This activity uses an actual recipe for a devil's food cake with marshmallow frosting. The original recipe serves eight people. Students, working together, change the recipe to bake enough cakes to feed their math class (or perhaps all of the students in the school).

5 × 5 PUZZLE CENTS

This is an activity that makes practice with addition of decimals entertaining. Students are able to manipulate "coins" by cutting out the squares and moving them around a grid. The coins become a readily available manipulative that encourages the development of problem-solving strategies.

CHOCOLATE CHIP COOKIES

In this activity, the cost of each ingredient is listed, and students are asked to find the cost of each cookie, how much profit could be made if they were sold, and what percentage the profit represents. The next best thing to eating these cookies is thinking about eating them!

MUSIC AND FRACTIONS

Students use their fractions skills in this real-world activity that makes connections between music and mathematics. By adding and subtracting notes, students employ a mathematical skill and experience a real-world application for using fractions.

MATHEMATICAL PALINDROMES

Palindromes have played a fascinating role in both language and mathematics. In addition to palindromic words and phrases, there are also palindromic numbers—the same whether they are read from left to right or right to left. An example of a palindromic number is 123321. Students have the opportunity to experiment with a technique that usually produces a palindromic number while they practice addition and collect some data for future discussion and analysis.

Musical Palindromes extends students' newly learned knowledge of music to a more creative realm—that of music writing. But this is music writing with a little twist—a musical piece that contains a palindromic sequence.

$1,000,000 LONG

TEACHER'S PLANNING INFORMATION

Math Topics

Numeration, estimation, computation with large numbers, problem solving, mathematical connections

Active Learning

Students will

1. Estimate the length of one million dollar bills

2. Work collaboratively to develop problem-solving strategies

3. Measure one bill and compute the length of one million bills

4. Convert their results to appropriate units of measure

5. Use a map to determine the distance

6. Discover important landmarks within a circle of a determined radius

Materials

Rulers; dollar bills; maps; calculators; $1,000,000 Long Worksheets

Suggestions for Instruction

Hold up a dollar bill and ask, "How long do you think one $1 bill is?" If all of the responses are written on the blackboard, the estimates can be used to do some statistical analysis. Students can be asked for the range, the mode, or the mean. If they are ordered, the median can be found. Once some statistical analysis is done, students can be asked if they wish to change their estimates or not.

Then ask, "If we placed one million of these end to end, how far do you think they would reach?" At this point, students should not be given the use of calculators. After some discussion, place students in pairs and give each pair of students one copy of the $1,000,000 Long Worksheet. Have each pair record its estimate on its worksheet in the space provided. To encourage mathematical reasoning, it is important for students to write a detailed explanation of where they could travel and how they calculated the distance.

- http://hypertextbook.com/facts/1999/Denene Williams.shtml contains information about not only the length of a $1 bill but also its thickness—it is 1/10 mm thick.

Selected Answers

A dollar bill is approximately 6.25 inches long, so it can be used as a handy benchmark to help one estimate the length of objects. One million would be approximately 6,250,000 inches, or 520,833.3 feet, or 98.6 miles long.

Variation

Give each group of students a map and have them find the area of a circle formed with a 98.6-mile radius and find all of the important cities or landmarks within that area. Also, if students go to the Web site cited previously, they can conduct an experiment to calculate how high a stack of one million dollar bills would be.

Writing in Math

Journal questions:

1. How far do you think $1 billion would reach? Explain your reasoning.

2. Now that you know the approximate length of a dollar bill, how might you use this information as a benchmark to help you estimate other distances?

$1,000,000 Long

Worksheet

Name _____

Date _____ Class _____

Directions: Work with your partner to problem solve how far one million one-dollar bills would reach if they were placed end to end. Do you think they would reach across a football field? Across your state? Across the United States? Across the world? Write your estimate here:

_____

Working with your partner, use a dollar bill, a ruler, and a calculator to determine how far one million bills would actually reach. Be sure to express your distance using reasonable units of measure. Write an explanation of your reasoning and calculations in the spaces that follow. Use a map to determine how far you could travel. Where could you go? How did you figure that out?

_____

_____

_____

_____

How does this answer compare with your initial estimate? How would you rate your estimate?

_____

_____

What other cities or landmarks fall within the calculated distance?

_____

_____

HOW MANY STRIDES TO WALK AROUND THE EARTH?

TEACHER'S PLANNING INFORMATION

Suggestions for Instruction

The distance around the Earth is 24,902 miles or 40,074 km. This activity does not direct students to measure using customary units or metric units. This is not an oversight. It is possible to use either system of measurement, depending on curricular needs. Whether customary or metric units are used, students will need to convert miles to feet or inches or kilometers to meters or centimeters.

Begin the activity by asking, "How many strides do you think you would take if you were to walk around the earth's equator?" It is important for students to understand that it takes two steps to form one stride. Demonstrate a two-step stride. Ask students if they believe this is a normal stride. Students should see that any one stride cannot be considered "normal"; multiple strides (20 or more) need to be taken and the total distance divided by the number of strides to find the average length of just one.

Place students in collaborative groups of four, give them the materials they need, and have them proceed to solve the problem. When group averages have been calculated, bring the class back together to find the length of an average stride for the class. Class results can be analyzed to find the range of the data, the mean, median, and mode, any outliers, and so forth.

A very interesting book to supplement this activity is Kathryn Lasky's (1994) *The Librarian Who Measured the Earth.* It tells the story of Eratosthenes (circa 200 BC), an ancient Greek librarian, who figured out how to calculate the circumference of the Earth by using the angles formed by the sun's shadows.

Math Topics

Numeration, estimation, computation with large numbers, measurement, problem solving with large numbers, averages, mathematical connections, reasoning

Active Learning

Students will

1. Work in groups of four to solve this problem

2. Problem solve the length of a normal stride

3. Accurately measure the length of their strides

4. Find the average or mean length of a stride for their group

5. Compute the number of "normal" strides it would take to walk around the Earth

6. Combine their group's data with the class's data to facilitate statistical analysis

Materials

Metersticks or yardsticks (or tapes); copies of How Many Strides to Walk Around the Earth? Worksheet 1; calculators; overhead transparency of How Many Strides to Walk Around the Earth? Worksheet 2

- http://www.lyberty.com/encyc/articles/earth.html shows students how the circumference of the Earth can be calculated using the formula $C = \pi d$.
- http://www.guinnessworldrecords.com/content_pages/record.asp?recordid=48612 tells the story of David Kunst who was the first verified person to walk around the world.

Variation

Have students compute the number of strides to walk to the moon (an average distance of 384,000 km or 239,000 mi).

Writing in Math

Journal questions:

1. Why did your group use the mean length of your strides to solve the problem?

2. It would take a train traveling 100 kph (161 mph) about 99.5 days to reach the moon. How long would you estimate it would take (on the average) for you to walk there?

How Many Strides to Walk Around the Earth?

Worksheet 1

Name _____

Date _____ Class _____

Suppose you went on a long hike around the earth's equator. How many strides would it take?

Directions: A stride is the distance you travel when walking two steps. For example, if you start walking with your left foot, when your right foot touches the ground, you have walked one stride. In your group, problem solve how you might find a normal stride for each member; then measure the length of a stride for each member of your group and enter these measurements on the table that follows. Find the mean (or average) length of one stride for the members of your group. But first, in the following space, describe what you will do to determine a "normal" stride.

_____

_____

_____

_____

Our Group Data

Name of Person	Length of Stride
Mean Length of Stride	

The distance around the Earth at the equator is about 40,000 km (40,000,000 m), or about 24,000 miles. About how many strides would it take to walk around the world? Use the stride length computed from your group's experiment.

How Many Strides to Walk Around the Earth?

Worksheet 2

Class Data Sheet

Group	Mean Length of Stride
Mean Length of Stride for Class	

Is there a difference between the mean for the length of a stride for individual groups and the whole class? If there is, why do you think this occurred? Write your answer on the back of this page.

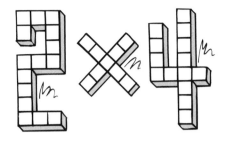

RECTANGLES AND FACTORS

TEACHER'S PLANNING INFORMATION

Suggestions for Instruction

Place students into pairs, provide them with the necessary manipulatives, and give them time to find the factors of each of the first 20 numbers. Each pair of students will need about 30 tiles.

To demonstrate the activity, place 12 tiles on the overhead projector and ask for student volunteers to place these tiles into rectangular arrays. Some possibilities are 1×12, 2×6, and 3×4. (For the purposes of this activity, a 1×12 and a 12×1 will be considered the same array.) The possibilities look like this:

3×4

2×6

1×12

Math Topics

Numeration, factors, area, prime and composite numbers, geometry

Active Learning

Students will

1. Work in pairs for this activity

2. Use manipulatives to form rectangles

3. Understand that the sides of these rectangles are factors of the area

4. Discover the difference between prime and composite numbers

Materials

Buckets of square tiles (cardboard tiles can be used), Rectangles and Factors Worksheets, overhead tiles for demonstration

Students will discover that prime numbers have only one rectangular array, whereas composite numbers have at least two.

Variation

Students can be encouraged to find the prime factors of each of the numbers and, using combinations, find the integral factors. For example, the prime factors of 12 are $2 \times 2 \times 3$; the combinations are 2^0, 2^1, 2^2, 3^1, $2^1 \times 3^1$, and $2^2 \times 3^1$. This activity gives them the opportunity to work with concrete materials and abstract concepts simultaneously.

Writing in Math

Journal questions:

1. Explain how the number of rectangles formed by the factors of a number can tell you whether the number is prime or composite.

2. Some of the numbers between 0 and 21 have an odd number of factors. How would you describe these numbers?

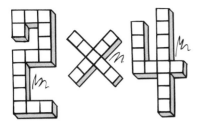

Rectangles and Factors

Worksheet

Name _____

Date _____ Class _____

Directions: Form rectangles using the number of tiles shown. Describe each of the rectangles in the space provided. Then record the factors for each rectangle.

Number of Tiles	Description of Rectangles (Length × Width)	List of Factors
1		
2		
3		
4		
5		
6		
7		
8		
9		
10		
11		
12		
13		
14		
15		
16		
17		
18		
19		
20		

Write your observations about the size of the rectangles and their factors on the back of this page.

VENN DIAGRAMS: LCM AND GCF

TEACHER'S PLANNING INFORMATION

Math Topics

Numeration, number theory, reasoning, Venn diagrams

Active Learning

Students will

1. Work in pairs to solve these problems

2. Find the prime factors of a pair of numbers

3. Place the factors correctly in a Venn diagram

4. Understand the relationship between the intersection of the sets and the GCF (greatest common factor)

5. Understand the relationship between the union of the sets and the LCM (least common multiple)

Materials

Venn Diagrams: LCM and GCF Worksheets

Suggestions for Instruction

This activity assumes that students understand how to find the prime factors of a number, perhaps by using factor trees. Venn diagrams are used in this activity to help students find the greatest common factor and least common multiple of two numbers.

Venn diagrams are named for the mathematician who developed them, John Venn. They have been used since the late 1800s. Venn diagrams are used to show the relationships between different elements in a set. For example, if we want to represent the set of students who are wearing red, blue, or both in class, our Venn diagram might look like this:

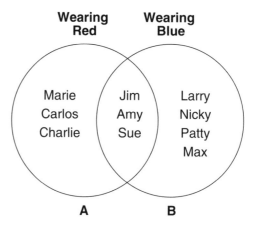

This diagram can be copied on the blackboard or on an overhead transparency, or one can be made using actual students. This simple diagram can be used to help explain the reasoning behind the placement within the diagram.

Some questions to ask students:

1. Who are all the students in this group? (This is the union of the two sets: A∪B.)

2. Who are the students wearing both red and blue? (This is the intersection of the two sets: A∩B.)

3. See how the circles overlap but not completely; why?

4. Where might we write the names of the students who are not wearing any red or blue?

After students understand the placement of members in a Venn diagram, give each pair of students a copy of the Venn Diagrams: LCM and GCF Worksheet. Read the directions with the students and be sure that they all understand how to find the prime factors of each of the numbers. Then explain how the numbers were placed in the Venn diagram shown on the worksheet.

Students can now work in pairs, following these steps: (1) choose two numbers, (2) find the prime factors of each number, (3) place the numbers correctly in the Venn diagram, and (4) find the union (LCM) and intersection (GCF) of the two numbers.

- http://www.teach-nology.com/web_tools/graphic_org/venn_diagrams/

  This is a Web site that will allow the teacher to create Venn diagrams for student use.

- http://www.shodor.org/interactivate/activities/vdiagram/index.html

  This is a wonderful interactive Web site that asks students where a particular item should be placed and then allows the student to know if the answer is correct or not. It includes questions about number theory, algebra, people, and so forth. It has very diverse offerings.

- http://www.stat.sc.edu/~west/applets/Venn.html

  This interesting interactive site shades in two rectangles (A and B). Students get to choose from the following: A, not A, B, not B, A and B, A or B, not (A and B), not (A or B). The site also indicates the geometric probability of each of these events based upon the area of each rectangle.

Variation

Expand the activity to include 3-circle Venn diagrams that examine the LCM and GCF of three numbers.

Writing in Math

Journal questions:

1. Describe the differences between these Venn diagrams: (6 and 8) and (8 and 24).

2. Can you think of two numbers where the circles would not overlap (have no intersection)?

Venn Diagrams:
LCM and GCF

Worksheet

Name _____

Date _____ Class _____

Directions:

1. Find the prime factors of your numbers.

2. When the two numbers share a factor, place that factor in the intersection of the two circles.

Remember: The intersection of the two circles is the GCF (greatest common factor). The union of the two circles is the LCM (least common multiple).

Example: Let's look at 12 and 16
The prime factors of 12 are $2 \times 2 \times 3$
The prime factors of 16 are $2 \times 2 \times 2 \times 2$
The intersection, 4, is the GCF
The union, 48, is the LCM

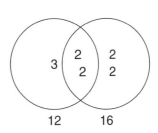

My two numbers are _____

Their prime factors are _____

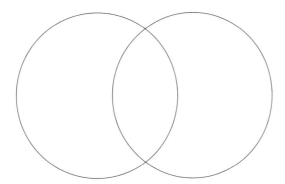

DESSERT FOR A CROWD

TEACHER'S PLANNING INFORMATION

Math Topics

Fractions, problem solving, connections

Active Learning

Students will

1. Work in pairs to solve an open-ended problem

2. Use fraction concepts and skills to solve a real-world problem

3. Convert a recipe to feed a larger number of people

Materials

Dessert for a Crowd Worksheets 1 and 2 for each pair of students

Suggestions for Instruction

Discuss with students how pastry chefs need to convert recipes to feed different numbers of people. You can use an example of a recipe that makes a cake that serves 12. If there are going to be 50 people at a party, the chef could convert the recipe in the following way:

$$\frac{50}{12} = 4\frac{1}{6}$$

The chef needs to have between four and five cakes. To make sure there is enough dessert, the chef will need to have five times the amount of each of the ingredients in the recipe.

Give each pair of students a copy of the original recipe. Read the directions with them and make sure they understand appropriate measurements (for example, can you have half an egg?). Make sure students agree on the number of students in the class. Suppose the class has 28 members. Students need to calculate the conversion factor, and that can be done in a number of ways:

An algebraic equation: $8n = 28$; where n represents the conversion factor

A ratio and proportion: $\dfrac{1 \text{ cake}}{8 \text{ people}} = \dfrac{n \text{ cakes}}{28 \text{ people}}$

A division problem: $28 \div 8 = 3.5$; the conversion factor is 4.

Place the students into pairs and have them problem solve how they will convert the amount of ingredients needed to serve eight people to the amount of ingredients needed to feed the number of students in the class. After each group has developed its own strategy, have them convert the recipe (including the directions) to feed the entire mathematics class.

- http://kmiller.ecorp.net/recipe/ is only one of the Web sites that has a calculator to calculate changes that need to be made in a recipe to feed a particular number of people. There are many other sites that will convert customary units to metric and metric to customary.

Variation

This recipe can be enlarged to feed the entire grade level or the entire school. The calculations become more difficult as the number of people to be fed is enlarged.

Writing in Math

Journal questions:

1. Explain the procedures (the strategies) you used to enlarge the recipe to feed the entire class.

2. How do you think your strategies would change if you needed to convert the recipe to feed four people instead of eight?

Dessert for a Crowd

Worksheet 1

Directions: The recipe for devil's food cake with marshmallow frosting will serve about eight people (each person will get 1/8 of the cake). Work with your partner to alter the recipe so that you can make enough cakes to feed the class. Be sure to rewrite the directions so that you will be making the correct number of cakes.

DEVIL'S FOOD CAKE

½ cup margarine

1½ cups sugar

1 egg

2 egg yolks

3 ounces unsweetened chocolate, melted and cooled

2 cups flour

1 teaspoon baking soda

¾ teaspoon salt

1 cup milk

1 teaspoon vanilla extract

Cream butter. Gradually add sugar and cream until light and fluffy. Add egg and egg yolks, one at a time, beating well after each addition. Add chocolate. Add dry ingredients alternately with milk. Add vanilla. Pour into two round 9-inch layer pans. Bake in a 350° oven for about 30 minutes. Cool and frost with marshmallow frosting.

MARSHMALLOW FROSTING

1½ cups sugar

⅓ cup water

¼ teaspoon salt

2 egg whites

1½ teaspoons corn syrup

1 teaspoon vanilla extract

16 (¼ pound) marshmallows, quartered

Combine all of the ingredients, except vanilla and marshmallows, in the top part of a double boiler. Beat for 7 minutes, or until stiff peaks form. Remove from heat and add vanilla and marshmallows.

Dessert for a Crowd

Worksheet 2

Name _____

Date _____ Class _____

Directions: Work with your partner to figure out the correct quantities of ingredients for this class. Make sure you have enough for every student and a piece for the teacher! Use the spaces provided to design your recipes.

DEVIL'S FOOD CAKE

_____ cup margarine

_____ cups sugar

_____ egg

_____ egg yolks

_____ ounces unsweetened
chocolate, melted and cooled

_____ cups flour

_____ teaspoon baking soda

_____ teaspoon salt

_____ cup milk

_____ teaspoon vanilla extract

Cream butter. Gradually add sugar and cream until light and fluffy. Add egg and egg yolks, one at a time, beating well after each addition. Add chocolate. Add dry ingredients alternately with milk. Add vanilla. Pour into _____ round 9-inch layer pans. Bake in a 350° oven for about 30 minutes. Cool and frost with marshmallow frosting.

MARSHMALLOW FROSTING

_____ cups sugar

_____ cup water

_____ teaspoon salt

_____ egg whites

_____ teaspoons corn syrup

_____ teaspoon vanilla extract

_____ marshmallows, quartered

Combine all of the ingredients, except vanilla and marshmallows, in the top part of a double boiler. Beat for 7 minutes, or until stiff peaks form. Remove from heat and add vanilla and marshmallows.

5 × 5 PUZZLE CENTS

TEACHER'S PLANNING INFORMATION

Math Topics

Decimals, problem solving

Active Learning

Students will

1. Use decimal skills to solve a puzzle

2. Work to find multiple solutions

Materials

Scissors, 5 × 5 Puzzle Cents Worksheets, calculators (if necessary)

Suggestions for Instruction

Students can work alone or in pairs. After cutting out the coins on the bottom of the worksheet, allow students time to solve the puzzle. By moving the tokens around, students will find it easier to try different possibilities. Sums give a clue to the numbers that belong in the blanks.

Selected Answers

A possible solution is shown below. There are other ways to solve this puzzle.

10¢	5¢	50¢	25¢	25¢
10¢	5¢	5¢	10¢	10¢
5¢	25¢	1¢	25¢	25¢
50¢	10¢	50¢	5¢	50¢
1¢	50¢	1¢	1¢	1¢

Variation

Students may be given the option of using calculators to solve the puzzle. Have students create their own puzzle for the rest of the class. Students can also work on magic squares where the sum of the numbers in each column, row, and diagonal add up to the same number. This is an example of a decimal magic square.

Directions: Use the numbers 0.2, 0.4, 0.6, 0.8, 1.0, 1.2, 1.4, 1.6, and 1.8 to make a magic square with a sum of 3.0. There are many solutions to this problem but one of them is shown below.

0.4	1.4	1.2
1.8	1.0	0.2
0.8	0.6	1.6

Writing in Math

Journal questions:

1. Explain why *lining up the decimal points* when adding decimals and *finding common denominators* when we add fractions speak about the same mathematics concept.

2. Explain whether the sums at the end of the rows helped you solve the problem. If you used another strategy, explain how it helped you solve the problem.

5 × 5 Puzzle Cents

Worksheet

Name _____

Date _____ Class _____

Placing one coin in each square, arrange five pennies, five nickels, five dimes, five quarters, and five half-dollars in this 5 × 5 grid so that the totals of each row and column equal the amount to the right of each row and under each column.

					$1.15
					$0.40
					$0.81
					$1.65
					$0.54
$0.76	**$0.95**	**$1.07**	**$0.66**	**$1.11**	

5 × 5 Puzzle Cents—Worksheet (Continued)

CHOCOLATE CHIP COOKIES

TEACHER'S PLANNING INFORMATION

Math Topics

Computation, problem solving, fractions, decimals, connections

Active Learning

Students will

1. Work with a partner to solve the problem

2. Compute the total cost of each of the ingredients

3. Compute the total cost of the cookie batter

4. Compute the cost of one cookie

5. Compute the profit and percentage of profit

Materials

Chocolate Chip Cookies Worksheets, calculators

Suggestions for Instruction

Discuss with students the mathematics of cooking! Ask them what math they think a chef or caterer might need to know. Students might say that chefs need to convert recipes or determine how much to charge for a meal. After students have had a chance to examine the worksheet, discuss the problem and why it is important to find the total cost of each of the ingredients in a recipe, regardless of the quantity needed. Students may need assistance in converting fractions to decimals and interpreting the answers. The cost of baking soda and salt is less than 1¢; this may pose difficulties for some students. These problems are challenging to solve because they combine the multiplication of fractions and decimals. In the first problem, students are asked to multiply the mixed number 4½ by the decimal 0.32. While it is possible for students to change the 32¢ to a fraction, they will most likely want to change the ½ to 0.5.

Have students work with a partner. After they find the total cost for each ingredient, they are asked to find the cost per cookie.

Selected Answers

The total cost for the ingredients is about $30.75; the cost per cookie is about 13¢; Depending on how the pairs rounded, the profit is about 290%.

Variation

Consumerism issues (i.e., percentage of profit) may be of great interest to students at this level. Interesting problems involve finding the cost per pound of cosmetics, perfume, or other very highly priced items. For example, suppose ground beef selling for $1.89/lb is used to make a ¼-pound hamburger. The cost for the meat is about 46¢. If the bun costs 10¢ and the rest of the ingredients add another 4¢, the total cost for the hamburger is about 60¢. If the restaurant sells it for $2.49, the percentage of profit is over 300%. But what other expenses does a restaurant owner have besides the cost of the ingredients used?

Writing in Math

Journal questions:

1. Explain how there can be a percentage greater than 100%. Give an example.

2. What would happen if a 25¢ cookie was sold for the price in your example?

Chocolate Chip Cookies

Worksheet

Name _____

Date _____ Class _____

Ingredient	Amount Needed for Recipe	Cost per Unit	Total Cost for Each Item
Margarine	4½ lbs.	$0.32/lb.	
Creamed Shortening	4½ lbs.	$0.48/lb.	
White Sugar	8½ lbs.	$0.31/lb.	
Brown Sugar	7 lbs.	$1.01/lb.	
Eggs	40	$0.08/ea.	
Vanilla (imitation)	½ cup	$0.40/cup	
Flour	16 lbs.	$0.15/lb.	
Baking Soda	6 tablespoons	$0.013/tablespoons	
Salt	6 tablespoons	$0.0017/tablespoons	
Chocolate Chips	9 lbs.	$2.56/lb.	
TOTAL COST			

Total amount of cookies: 240 at a cost of _____ ea.

If the cookies are sold at 50¢ each, how much profit would be made?

_____

What is the percentage of profit?

_____

_____

MUSIC AND FRACTIONS

TEACHER'S PLANNING INFORMATION

Suggestions for Instruction

While some students will have studied music and are familiar with what the notes look like and how fractions are used to keep time, many may not have. Worksheet 1 gives a brief explanation of the value of each note and the rests. It explains how music is written and that a "$\frac{4}{4}$" in the signature indicates that each measure contains four beats, and a quarter note is given one beat. Any combination of notes can be used to add up to four beats. A whole note is worth four beats, a half note is worth two beats, a quarter note is worth one beat, an eighth note is worth one-half a beat, and so on. The notes look like this:

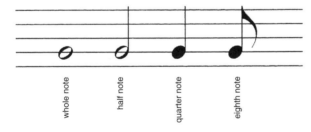

Math Topics

Fraction concepts, problem solving, connections

Active Learning

Students will

1. Work in pairs to make connections between music and mathematics

2. Learn the value of musical notes and rests

3. Add fractions to complete the value of measures

4. Subtract fractions to find the difference in the value of notes

5. Complete the value of measures by filling in missing notes and rests

Materials

Music and Fractions Worksheets 1–4

Variation

Students should be encouraged to develop their own fill-in-the-note activities.

Writing in Math

Journal questions:

1. Describe what fractions and music have in common. Explain your answer.

2. You are playing a piece of music that is written in $\frac{3}{4}$ time. What information do you get from the numerator? What information do you get from the denominator?

Music and Fractions

Worksheet I

Name _____

Date _____ Class _____

The music at the right is written in four-four time, meaning that a quarter note counts as one beat and there are four beats to a measure. Each of the notes pictured is a square note: $\frac{1}{4} + \frac{1}{4} + \frac{1}{4} + \frac{1}{4} = \frac{4}{4} = 1$.

In each measure of a piece of music, the sum of all of the notes will always equal 1! Can you believe it? There are fractions even in music! Look at the explanation of the notes that follows. It shows you what the notes look like and how much they are worth. A dotted note is equal to the value of the note plus one-half the value of the note. For example, a dotted half-note equals $\frac{1}{2} + \frac{1}{4}$ or $\frac{3}{4}$.

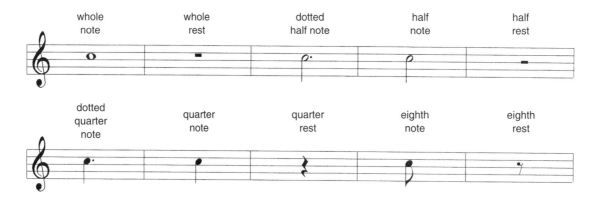

Can you calculate the values of these notes?

Music and Fractions

Worksheet 2

Name _____

Date _____ Class _____

Fill in the Note

Each measure of a musical piece has a value of one. The measures that follow have something missing—they don't add up to one. For example, the first measure contains only two one-fourth notes, meaning the measure has a value of only one-half. Your job is to complete the measure so that it has a value of one by using only **one note**. You may use the value chart to help you solve these problems.

Fill in the Rest

Sometimes rests (where we count a beat but do not play a note) are used to complete a measure. Complete the following measures by using only one rest.

Music and Fractions

Worksheet 3

Adding Rhythms

Write the answer to each of these addition problems using only one note.

$$♫ + ♩ =$$

$$♫ + ♩ =$$

$$♩. + ♫ =$$

$$♩ + ♪ =$$

$$♩ + ♩ + ♫ =$$

$$♩. + ♪ =$$

$$♫ + ♫ + ♫ =$$

Music and Fractions

Worksheet 4

Subtracting Rhythms

Write the answer to each of these subtraction problems using only one note.

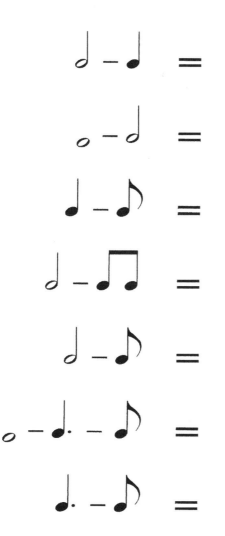

MATHEMATICAL PALINDROMES

TEACHER'S PLANNING INFORMATION

Suggestions for Instruction

Discuss with students interesting palindromes from literature. Palindromes can be words, numbers, or even musical notes. Words such as *racecar*, *reviver*, and *rotator* can be written the same backward and forward. A famous palindrome, "A man, a plan, a canal—Panama!," is the epitaph of Ferdinand de Lesseps, who was associated with the famous canal. We even have whole sentences, such as an amazing one written in 1967 by James Michie: "Doc note, I dissent. A fast never prevents a fatness. I diet on cod." There are even tongue twisters, such as Leigh Mercer's: "Top steps pup's pet spot."

Ask students to work in pairs to discover interesting phrases or sentences that are palindromes. Now look at the examples of number palindromes given at the beginning of Worksheet 1.

Read the directions with students and explain the reverse-and-add method of changing numbers into palindromes. Have each pair of students choose a number, use the reverse-and-add method to change it to a palindrome, and share their palindrome with the class.

Give students time to complete the table and the assignment.

The Internet is jam-packed with sites about palindromes:

- http://www.palindromelist.com/

  This is a huge list that is listed alphabetically.

- http://www.fun-with-words.com/palindromes.html

  This is a very interesting site that, in addition to traditional palindromes, has palindromic squares.

- http://www.derf.net/palindromes/old.palindrome.html#POEMS

Math Topics

Computation, problem solving, data collection

Active Learning

Students will

1. Work collaboratively to find a word, phrase, or sentence that is a palindrome

2. Convert numbers into palindromes by following a described procedure

3. Problem solve to find their own one-step, two-step, and three-step number palindromes

4. Extend the concept of palindromes to include a musical piece that is palindromic

Materials

Mathematical Palindromes Worksheets 1–3; markers, crayons, or colored pencils

This is a continuation of a much larger site—this section contains some palindromic poems. These poems are the same when they are read from top to bottom (left to right) as they are when read from bottom to top (right to left). Fascinating!

Variation

You may use the additional sheet, More Mathematical Palindromes, and have students color code the grid based on the number of steps it takes to convert numbers to palindromes. Can they find a pattern?

Writing in Math

Journal questions:

1. Choose a number and use the reverse-and-add method to convert it to a palindromic number.

2. Why do you think the reverse-and-add method works? Explain your reasoning.

Mathematical Palindromes

Worksheet 1

Name _____

Date _____ Class _____

A palindrome is a word, sentence, or number that is the same forward and backward. *Racecar* and *A man, a plan, a canal—Panama!* are examples of palindromic words and phrases. Write down your own example of a word, sentence, or phrase that is a palindrome:

_____

_____

An example of a palindromic number is 1234321. We even have dates that are palindromic, for example, 1881. What was the first palindromic date in the 21st century? What will the next one be?

_____

_____

We can turn numbers into palindromes by following some simple arithmetic steps:

1. Write down the original number

2. Reverse the digits

3. Add the original number to the number reversed

If you have a palindrome, you are finished; if you don't, continue the process of reverse-and-add until you have a palindrome. Here are some examples:

38 + 83 ――― 121	This is a one-step palindrome.	156 + 651 ――― 807 + 708 ――― 1515 + 5151 ――― 6666	This is a three-step palindrome. Reverse and add. Reverse and add.

Mathematical Palindromes—Worksheet 1 (Continued)

There are 24 steps to getting a palindrome from the number 89. The palindrome is 8,813,200,023,188. It appears that the number 196 does not have a palindrome. Complete this table and record the number of steps and the resulting palindrome:

Number	Number of Steps	Palindrome
148		
59		
364		
352		
85		
785		

Work with your partner to develop one-step, two-step, and three-step palindromes. They are:

One step: _____

Two step: _____

Three step: _____

Mathematical Palindromes

Worksheet 2

Name _____

Date _____ Class _____

The table to the right contains the numbers from 10–139. Work with your partner to convert these to palindromes. Follow these directions:

10	11	12	13	14	15	16	17	18	19
20	21	22	23	24	25	26	27	28	29
30	31	32	33	34	35	36	37	38	39
40	41	42	43	44	45	46	47	48	49
50	51	52	53	54	55	56	57	58	59
60	61	62	63	64	65	66	67	68	69
70	71	72	73	74	75	76	77	78	79
80	81	82	83	84	85	86	87	88	89
90	91	92	93	94	95	96	97	98	99
100	101	102	103	104	105	106	107	108	109
110	111	112	113	114	115	116	117	118	119
120	121	122	123	124	125	126	127	128	129
130	131	132	133	134	135	136	137	138	139

1. If it is already a palindrome, leave it uncolored.

2. If you can convert it into a palindrome in one step, color it yellow.

3. If you need two steps to change it into a palindrome, color it green.

4. If you need three steps to change it into a palindrome, color it red.

5. If you need four or more steps to change it into a palindrome, color it blue.

Do you see a pattern?

Explain: _____

_____

_____

_____

_____

_____

What fractional part of your chart is

1. Uncolored? _____

2. Yellow? _____

3. Green? _____

4. Red? _____

5. Blue? _____

Mathematical (and Musical) Palindromes

Worksheet 3

Name _____

Date _____ Class _____

If we can have number palindromes, why can't we have musical palindromes? This would be a tune that is the same whether we play it forward or backward. An example of a musical palindrome follows. The blank musical staffs after the example are for you and your partner to use to create your own musical palindrome.

Active Algebra 2

Active Algebra 2

The human mind has never invented a labor-saving machine equal to algebra.

—Author Unknown

In *Principles and Standards for School Mathematics*, the National Council of Mathematics (2000) recommends that all students—from primary school through high school—learn algebra concepts. The council suggests that students should (1) understand patterns and functions; (2) use algebraic symbols; (3) learn to use graphs, tables, and equations; and (4) understand how graphs can be used to represent change. In *Algebra for Everyone*, the NCTM (1990) states, "Algebra is a universal theme that runs through all of mathematics, and it is a tool required by nearly all aspects of our nations' economy" (p. v).

While teachers often hear, "When am I ever going to use this?" in their algebra classes, it is hoped that by utilizing motivating activities, different learning styles, interesting puzzles, and applications to real-world data, students can find algebra class an interesting place to be.

PATTERNS, PATTERNS, PATTERNS

This activity encourages students to progress from using hands-on, concrete manipulatives to drawing two-dimensional representations and finally to generalizing the pattern using algebraic expression. Once students become familiar with the mathematics behind these growing patterns, they can be encouraged to design a Class Pattern Book. The patterns can be made using pattern blocks, but if these are not available, sheets of square tiles and triangles are provided.

ALGEBRA JOKES

The puzzle sheets in this activity provide a motivating, self-correcting review of linear equations and geometric measurement. The equations in the first three jokes become increasingly more difficult. To solve the forth puzzle, students need to have prior knowledge about the measurement of degrees in triangles and quadrilaterals. When students find the sum of the algebraic expressions that define the number of degrees in each angle, they discover the letters that are needed to find the punch line. The jokes may be corny, but each punch line relates to something mathematical, so they aren't all bad.

THE M&M's MYSTERY

For this *delicious* data collection activity students secretly (1) find the total number of M&M's in their "Fun Size" bags and (2) assign algebraic expressions to represent each of the six colors. For example, if the number of green M&M's is defined as x and there are four more red than green, then the red ones can be defined as "$x + 4$." Once each student has assigned an algebraic expression to each color, he or she trades problems with a partner. Neither student knows anything more than the total number of candies in their partner's bag and the expression that defines the amount of each of the colors. By setting up equations and finding the sum of the expressions, students discover how many of each color their partners had in their bags. The activity ends with each partner making a circle graph of the data—and perhaps eating some of the M&M's.

ALGEBRA MATCH

In this activity, students are given a story problem, its equation, and its solution. Making connections between a verbal problem and its abstract equation can be very difficult for some middle school students. By cutting out each of the 18 parts and realigning them on a solution grid, students get to experiment and tactilely experience their options. When they are secure with their solutions, they glue it onto the solution grid.

INEQUALITY–NUMBER–LINE MATCH

Similar to the Algebra Match activity, students are required to correctly match an inequality (written in words), the algebraic expression for the inequality, and the graphic solution. Each of the 18 clues is cut out and can be moved around on the solution grid until all of the matches are found.

MIND READING OR ALGEBRA?

Students are asked to pick a number and perform a series of computations. Magically, the teacher knows the answer! This activity has amused and motivated students through the ages. Students are given a table that asks them to convert verbal clues to arithmetic problems and finally, to an algebraic format. By organizing the problem in this manner, students receive the help they need to make the important transition from the concrete numbers of arithmetic to abstract expressions of algebra. Students are then given the opportunity to develop their own mind-reading puzzles and share them with the class.

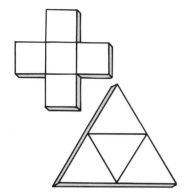

PATTERNS, PATTERNS, PATTERNS

TEACHER'S PLANNING INFORMATION

Suggestions for Instruction

The purpose behind using geometric patterns with students is to encourage an understanding of the power of algebra and finding the functional relationship between the number of the term and the outcome. When students are entering numbers in the table, they should be encouraged to look for the relationship between the input number and the output rather than using the number pattern that results from moving horizontally across the table. While seeing the horizontal pattern works for a limited number of terms, it is a useless strategy when asked to generalize to find the 50th figure, the 100th figure or the *n*th figure.

Open-ended problems are those that have more than one solution or those that have only one solution that can be arrived at in many different ways. Since many of the algebraic expressions that represent these patterns can be expressed in a variety of ways, it is very important to ask two questions: (1) Did anyone get a different answer? and (2) Did anyone solve this in a different way?

If triangular pattern blocks and square tiles are available, each pair of students will need about 30 square tiles and about 40 triangles. If these manipulatives are not available, sheets of triangles and tiles are available at the end of the lesson. If these are run off on card stock, laminated, and cut out, they will serve students just as well as commercially made manipulatives.

This activity is similar to those that have function machines, where the input and output are given and the function needs to be discovered. An interactive site called "Function Machine" can be located at http://www.shodor.org/interactivate/activities/fm/index.html.

Another area of this same Web site asks students to discover the pattern: http://www.shodor.org/interactivate/activities/patterns/index.html.

http://www.learner.org/channel/courses/learningmath/algebra/, the Learning Channel site, includes 10 different sessions: Algebraic Thinking,

Math Topics

Patterns, finding the formula for the *n*th pattern

Active Learning

Students will

1. Work in pairs to visualize geometric patterns
2. Make conjectures about resulting patterns
3. Arrive at conclusions based on their observations of a pattern
4. Use hands-on manipulatives to problem solve

Materials

One sheet each of tiles and triangles per pair of students; Worksheets 1, 2, and 3

Patterns in Context, Functions and Algorithms, Proportional Reasoning, Linear Functions and Slope, Solving Equations, and more. It is an interesting site to return to for more advanced problem solving.

Selected Answers

Students may have discovered the patterns using different strategies. The strategies shown are not the only possible answers.

Worksheet 1: Each figure will have the same number of squares on the bottom as the number of the figure and one less on the side—so the 10th figure will have 10 squares on the bottom and 9 on the side—for a total of 19. The 20th figure will have $20 + 19$ or 39; the 100th will have $100 + 99$. One way the formula for the nth figure could be written is $2n-1$.

Worksheet 2: There will be the same number of white triangles at the base of the figure as the number of the figure—so there will be seven white triangles at the base of Figure 7. There will be six (or one less) black triangles at that base. As you go up the triangle, there will be one less triangle on each row: $7 + 6 + 5 + 4 + 3 + 2 + 1$ white triangles and $6 + 5 + 4 + 3 + 2 + 1$ black triangles.

Worksheet 3: There will be 10 squares in the fourth pattern and 13 squares in the fifth pattern. There are many different strategies students can use to find the missing patterns. Give each pair of students the opportunity to share their solutions and the method they used to solve the pattern.

Variation

Students can be placed into groups of four, given a set of manipulatives, and assigned the task of designing their own geometric pattern. After solving the growth pattern for the first six patterns, they must determine what the 50th, the 100th, and the nth pattern will look like. Then they can share their pattern with other groups. Eventually a class book of geometric patterns can be published.

Writing in Math

Journal questions:

1. Look at this table of patterns:

Figure	1	2	3	4	20	50	100	n
Number of Squares	1	3	5	7				

Reading across the number of squares, you can see that two is added on each time. Why is this not helpful to find the number of squares in the 50th figure, the 100th figure, of the nth figure?

2. Find the 20th, the 50th, the 100th, and the nth figure in this pattern. Explain how you solved this problem.

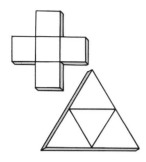

Patterns, Pattern, Patterns

Worksheet I

Name _____

Date _____ Class _____

Directions: If this pattern continues, what do you think the next three patterns will look like? After you discuss this with your partner, draw the next three patterns. Enter the number of squares in the table.

```
  □       □          □             □
         □ □        □ □           □ □
                    □ □ □         □ □
                                  □ □ □ □
  1       2          3             4          _____      _____      _____
                                               5             6             7
```

A table such as this one will help organize the information and help find the pattern.

Figure	1	2	3	4	5	6	7	10	20	100	n
Number of Squares	1	3	5	7							

1. How many squares will be in the 10th figure? _____ Describe what it will look like.

_____

2. How many will there be in the 20th figure? _____ In the 100th figure? _____

3. How many squares will there be in the nth figure? _____ Explain how you solved this pattern.

_____

_____

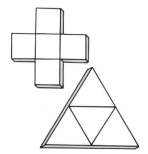

Patterns, Pattern, Patterns

Worksheet 2

Name _____

Date _____ Class _____

Directions: If this pattern continues, what do you think the next two patterns will look like? After you discuss this with your partner, draw the next two patterns.

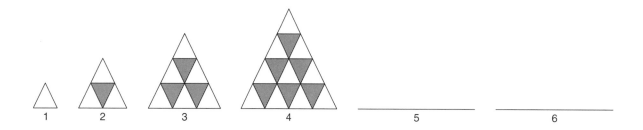

A table such as this one will help organize the information and help find the pattern between the number of white triangles and the number of black triangles.

| Number of White Triangles | 1 | 3 | 6 | 10 | | |
| Number of Black Triangles | 0 | 1 | 3 | 6 | | |

1. How many white triangles will there be at the base of the 7th figure? _____

2. How many black triangles will there be at the base of the 7th figure? _____

3. Can you problem solve how many rows of triangles there will be in the 7th figure? _____

4. How can you use this information to help you figure out how many triangles of each there will be in a figure of any size?

    _____

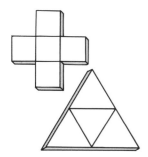

Patterns, Pattern, Patterns

Worksheet 3

Name _____

Date _____ Class _____

Directions: If this pattern continues, what do you think the next two patterns will look like? After you discuss this with your partner, draw the next two patterns. Enter the number of squares in the table.

1   2   3   4   5

A table such as this one will help organize the information and help find the pattern.

Figure	1	2	3	4	5	10	20	100	n
Number of Squares	1	4	7						

1. How many squares will be in the 10th figure? _____ Describe what it will look like.

    _____

2. How many will there be in the 20th figure? _____ In the 100th figure?

    _____

3. How many squares will there be in the nth figure? _____ Explain how you solved this pattern.

    _____

    _____

ALGEBRA JOKES

TEACHER'S PLANNING INFORMATION

Math Topics

Solving equations with one variable, computation

Active Learning

Students will

1. Solve a puzzle with one-variable equations

2. Solve problems where the variable appears on both sides of the equation

3. Solve equations correlated to the size of the angles of triangles and quadrilaterals

4. Work in groups of four to design an original Joke Puzzle

Materials

Joke Puzzle sheets 1–4 for each student

Suggestions for Instruction

The problems in these puzzles have been designed to give students experience with a variety of different equations. Puzzles vary in level of difficulty, but students have the advantage of having the answers at the end of each puzzle, so they are self-correcting. Students work with a partner, thereby sharing their skills.

Selected Answers

Algebra Joke 1: The answer to the question is "AN ALGEBRA PROBLEM."

Algebra Joke 2: The answer to the question is "A HIGH POT IN USE."

Algebra Joke 3: The answer to the question is "NINE: TREE PLUS TREE PLUS TREE."

Algebra Joke 4: The answer to the question is "PROBABLY."

Variation

Puzzles related to other math topics can be designed by students, collected, and then placed in a class puzzle book.

Writing in Math

Journal questions:

1. You solve an equation and your answer is $(-x) = 5$. How would you find the value of x as positive?

2. Explain how you solve a problem that has a fraction as a coefficient.

Algebra Joke 1

Name _____

Date _____ Class _____

QUESTION: What do you get if you add 2 apples and 3 oranges?

Directions: Solve each algebra problem. Show your work in the box. To find the answer to the question, write the *letter* of the problem in the correct space in the puzzle. If the answer appears in more than one place, write the letter of the problem in each of the spaces.

G	M	B	E	N
$2x + 5 = 13$	$5y - 8 = 2$	$3 + 2p = 13$	$s + 4 = 11$	$\frac{x}{3} = 6$
L	**R**	**A**	**P**	**O**
$3t - 1 = 26$	$9x = 27$	$7y - 3 = 53$	$46 - 2x = 22$	$2q - 3 = q + 3$

8	18		8	9	4	7	5	3	8		12	3	6	5	9	7	2

Algebra Joke 2

Name _____

Date _____ Class _____

QUESTION: What do you call a boiling pot that's on the top of Mt. Everest?

Directions: Solve each algebra problem. Show your work in the box. To find the answer to the question, write the *letter* of the problem in the correct space in the puzzle. If the answer appears in more than one place, write the letter of the problem in each of the spaces.

N	E	A	T	G
$25 = 3x + 4$	$30 - 4y = 6$	$6n - 8 = 3n + 1$	$x + 2x = 27$	$4 = \frac{x}{2}$

S	O	U	H	I
$y - 4 = 3y - 30$	$9x + 2 = 20$	$5n + 32 = 12n + 25$	$2q - 3 = q + 1$	$5x - x = 2x + 10$

P				
$p = 4p - 36$				

3		4	5	8	4		12	2	9		5	7		1	13	6

Algebra Joke 3

Name _____

Date _____ Class _____

QUESTION: What quantity does this represent:

Directions: Solve each algebra problem. Show your work in the box. To find the answer to the question, write the *letter* of the problem in the correct space in the puzzle. If the answer appears in more than one place, write the letter of the problem in each of the spaces.

S	T	P	N	I
$3S + 4 = S + 16$	$32 = 5T - 18$	$P + 2P + 3 = 30$	$N + 4 = 11$	$4I + 6 = 2I + 36$
E	**U**	**R**	**L**	
$E + 9 = 2E + 6$	$4U + 12 = 5U + 7$	$2R + 18 = 40$	$20 - 2L = 12$	

7	15	7	3		10	11	3	3		9	4	5	6		10	11	3	3		9	4	5	6		10	11	3	3

Algebra Joke 4

Name _____

Date _____ Class _____

QUESTION: Do you know any statistics jokes?

Directions: Solve each algebra problem. Show your work in the box. To find the answer to the question, write the *letter* of the problem in the correct space in the puzzle. The letter represents the value of "*x*." If the answer appears in more than one place, write the letter of the problem in each of the spaces. Please note: These angles have not been measured or drawn to scale.

A	P	Y
triangle: $3x°$, $x°$, $2x°$	parallelogram: $x°$, $3x°$	triangle: $(x + 10)°$, $(3x − 30)°$, $x°$
R	L	O
figure: $(4x + 5)°$, $x°$, right angle	triangle: $x°$, $x°$, $10x°$	quadrilateral: $25°$, $x°$, $(x − 55)°$, $(x − 60)°$
B		
triangle: $x°$, $(x − 110)°$, $(x − 100)°$		

45°	35°	150°	130°	30°	130°	15°	40°

THE M&M'S MYSTERY

TEACHER'S PLANNING INFORMATION

Suggestions for Instruction

Most of the activities that students have done using M&M's involve estimation, counting, and data collection. This activity is a little different. Students are asked to assign algebraic expressions to identify the quantity of each color of M&M's they have in their bags. To get them started, it is a good idea to run through the activity with a class demonstration. Let's assume that after opening your demonstration bag of M&M's, you have the following colors:

Orange: 5; Red: 2; Brown: 4; Blue: 6; Green: 3; and Yellow: 7

Say, "We will assign the variable "c" to the number of orange M&M's in this bag. There are 3 less red than orange. What expression can we use to make known the number of red?" Continue, giving students clues such as, "There is one less brown than orange" or "There are two more yellow than orange" and so on. When all of the colors have been defined by an expression, tell students the total number of M&M's in the package and ask them to set up an equation.

Math Topics

Variables, expressions, equations, problem solving, graphing

Active Learning

Students will

1. Find the number of each color of M&M's in their partner's bag using algebra

2. Assign algebraic expressions to represent the number of each color of M&M's

3. Trade their expressions with their partners

4. Solve the mystery by finding the number of each color their partners have

5. Design a circle graph to represent their partners' data

Materials

"Fun Size" bag of M&M's for each student, protractors, rulers, colored pencils or markers

Demonstration Bag of M&M's

Color	Number	Expression
Orange		c
Red		$c - 3$
Brown		$c - 1$
Blue		$c + 1$
Green		$c - 2$
Yellow		$c + 2$
TOTAL	27	

Once all the students have changed the number of each color to an algebraic expression, the table is given to their partners to problem solve the number of each color in their partners' bags of M&M's. If a student were using the foregoing information, the equation would be

$$c + c - 3 + c - 1 + c + 1 + c - 2 + c + 2 = 27$$

$$6c - 3 = 27$$

$$6c = 30$$

$$c = 5$$

Explain to students that once the value of "c" is known (5), it can be substituted in the other expressions and the number of each color of M&M's in their partners' bags can be calculated.

Give each student a small bag of M&M's and caution them to hide what's in the bag so that their partner will have an actual mystery to solve. Before they give their partners the partially completed tables, they must write (1) their expressions for each color in the table and (2) the total number of M&M's they have in their bags so the other student can set up an equation as shown in the foregoing table.

Selected Answers

Answers will vary since each child has developed his or her own set of variables.

Variation

As a class project, students can use a 5.3 oz. or a 9.4 oz. bag of M&M's. Using this larger size, students can calculate the percentage of each color there is in the bag and then, if computers are available, go to the M&M's Web site (http://us.mms.com/us/about/products/milkchocolate/) to see how close to the actual percentages their data is. This Web site has posted the new percentages for each of the colors of M&M's that are manufactured. The percentages have changed a great deal over the years. As of this writing, they are Brown: 13%; Yellow: 14%; Red: 13%; Blue: 24%; Orange: 20%; and Green: 16%. There is also some interesting nutritional information on this Web site.

Writing in Math

Journal questions:

1. Explain why it is possible for two students who have the same number of each color of M&M's to have different expressions to represent the colors.

2. Explain how you calculated the number of degrees required for each of the pie-shaped sections of your circle graph.

The M&M's Mystery

Worksheet 1

Name _____

Date _____ Class _____

This activity is a *mystery* because instead of recording the number of M&M's in your own bag, you are going to use your partner's algebraic expressions to figure out how many of each color your partner has.

Your partner has done these two things:

1. Written the expression for each color in the second column of this data sheet
2. Told you the total number of M&M's in his or her bag

You need to do these three things:

1. Use the expressions to set an equation
2. Write the number of each color you have calculated
3. Draw a graph to represent the data

M&M's Data Collection Table

Color	Expression	Number
Orange		
Red		
Brown		
Blue		
Green		
Yellow		
TOTAL # OF M&M's		

Show your work on the back of this page.

The M&M's Mystery

Worksheet 2

Name _____

Date _____ Class _____

Circle Graph Data

Directions: Complete the data table and use the information to draw a circle graph of the number of each color in your partner's bag of M&M's.

Color	Number	Percent	Degrees in Circle
Orange			
Red			
Brown			
Blue			
Green			
Yellow			
Totals			

Title of Graph:

_____

ALGEBRA MATCH

TEACHER'S PLANNING INFORMATION

Suggestions for Instruction

This activity requires students to read an equation, find the matching equation written in symbols, and match both of these to the answer. Each pair of students will need to cut out each of the three parts of the problem and then glue them on to the solution table.

Some students may need to review vocabulary, such as *sum, difference, product*, and *quotient*. They may also need refreshing on strategies to use when there is a fraction in an equation.

Pairs of students are asked to write an original Algebra Match problem. These can be collected and used as a class puzzle book.

Variation

Students can write Algebra Matches Problems using inequalities, such as, "When two is added to my number, the answer is greater than six and less than 8: $6 < x + 2 > 8; 7$."

Writing in Math

Journal questions:

1. List all of the math vocabulary words you needed to know to translate the story problem into an equation. Define the words.

2. Explain how you would solve an equation that contains a fraction.

Math Topics

Linear equations, reading mathematics

Active Learning

Students will

1. Work with a partner to read a linear equation

2. Match the story problem with the mathematical equation

3. Solve each equation and find its matching answer

4. Write an original Algebra Match problem to contribute to a class problem book

Materials

One Algebra Match Worksheet and one grid per pair of students, glue, scissors

Selected Answers

Solutions

The sum of one-third of a number and four is equal to eight.	$\frac{x}{3} + 4 = 8$	12
This number is the quotient when sixteen is divided by seven.	$\frac{16}{7} = n$	$2.\overline{2857142}$
Six less than twice this number is equal to thirty-eight.	$2x - 6 = 38$	22
Four more than twice this number equals thirty-eight.	$2x + 4 = 38$	17
The difference between six and twice this number is two.	$6 - 2x = 2$	2
Sixteen less than a number equals seven.	$n - 16 = 7$	23

Algebra Match

Worksheet

Directions: Cut out each of these sections. Then glue the problems, equations, and answers on the same line.

Story Problems

The sum of one-third of a number and four is equal to eight.	This number is the quotient when sixteen is divided by seven.	Six less than twice this number is equal to thirty-eight.
Four more than twice this number equals thirty-eight.	The difference between six and twice this number is two.	Sixteen less than a number equals seven.

Equations

$6 - 2x = 2$	$2x - 6 = 38$	$\dfrac{16}{7} = n$
$n - 16 = 7$	$\dfrac{x}{3} + 4 = 8$	$2x + 4 = 38$

Solutions

12	17	22
23	2	$2.\overline{2857142}$

Algebra Match

Solution Grid

Name _____

Date _____ Class _____

Directions: Match the problem, equation, and solution on the same line of this grid.

Story Problem	Equation	Solution

INEQUALITY NUMBER LINE MATCH

TEACHER'S PLANNING INFORMATION

Suggestions for Instruction

In this activity, the same expression is shown using three different representations: as a word problem, as an algebraic expression, and as a line graph. Students are asked to cut out each, match them, and glue them on to the Solution Grid page.

Some students may need to review the reasons some of the circles are open (indicating that the numbers are greater than or less than but not equal to) and some are closed (indicating that the numbers are greater than or equal to or less than or equal to). It may also be necessary to review the symbols used for the terms *less than, greater than, less than or equal to,* and *greater than or equal to.*

Variation

If students are working on graphing linear equations, the same type of matching activity can be used to represent the written problem, the equation, and the graphed line.

Writing in Math

Journal questions:

1. Explain why some inequality number line graphs have an open circle on the coordinate and some have a closed circle. Give an example of when each of these would be used.

2. Draw two number lines, indicate the coordinates, and graph this inequality: $-6 \leq x < 2$. Write the story problem for this inequality.

Math Topics

Graphing inequality expressions, problem solving

Active Learning

Students will

1. Work with a partner to problem solve

2. Match word problems with algebraic expressions and number line graphs

3. Recognize different representations of the same expression

Materials

One copy of the Inequality Number Line Match Worksheet and the Solution Grid for each pair of students, scissors, glue

Selected Answers

x is greater than or equal to one.	$x \geq 1$	
x is less than or equal to zero.	$x \leq 0$	
x is greater than zero.	$x > 0$	
x is greater than or equal to negative two and less than four.	$-2 \leq x < 4$	
x is greater than negative one and less than or equal to three.	$-1 < x \leq 3$	
x is greater than four or less than negative two.	$x > 4$ or $x < -2$	

Inequality Number Line Match

Worksheet

Name _____

Date _____ Class _____

Directions: Cut out each of these sections. Then glue the problems, equations, and answers on the same line.

Word Problems

x is greater than or equal to one	x is less than or equal to zero	x is less greater than zero
x is greater than or equal to negative two and less than four.	x is greater than negative one and less than or equal to three.	x is greater than four or less than negative two.

Inequalities

$x \leq 0$	$-1 < x \leq 3$	$x > 4$ or $x < -2$
$-2 \leq x < 4$	$x \geq 1$	$x > 0$

Graphs

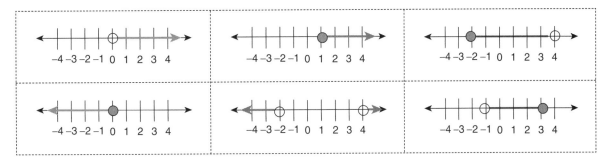

Inequality Number Line Match

Solution Grid

Name _____

Date _____ Class _____

Directions: Cut out each of these sections. Then glue the problems, equations, and answers on the same line.

Story Problem	Equation	Solution

MIND READING OR ALGEBRA?

TEACHER'S PLANNING INFORMATION

Suggestions for Instruction

This activity is designed to help students to see how algebra generalizes arithmetic. Problems such as the ones in this activity fascinate students and encourage them to see the value of algebra, as a generalization of arithmetic, in problem solving.

You can begin the lesson by reading the following two problems to students (the algebraic expressions in parentheses are to be shared with the students after both problems are read and students are interested in finding the "trick" to solve these problems).

Problem A:

1. Pick a number	(n)
2. Add 5	$(n + 5)$
3. Multiply by 2	$[2(n + 5) = 2n + 10]$
4. Subtract 10	$(2n + 10 - 10 = 2n)$
5. Divide by the number you started with	$\left(\dfrac{2n}{n}\right)$
6. Your answer is 2.	

Problem B:

1. Pick a number	(n)
2. Add the number you picked	$(n + n = 2n)$
3. Subtract 4	$(2n - 4)$
4. Multiply by 2	$[2(2n - 4) = 4n - 8]$
4. Multiply by $\frac{1}{4}$	$\left[\dfrac{1}{4}(4n - 8) = n - 2\right]$
5. Add 2	$(n - 2 + 2 = n)$
6. You're back to the number you started with (n).	

Math Topics

Algebraic expressions, problem solving

Active Learning

Students will

1. Read word clues and translate them into algebraic expressions
2. Work with partners to design their own algebra puzzles

Materials

One copy of Mind Reading or Algebra? puzzle sheet and one copy of Mind Reading or Algebra?—Make Up Your Own Worksheet for each pair of students

Now is the teachable moment! Repeat the problems again, but this time, write the algebraic expressions that are defined by the word phrases. These are written in parentheses next to each of the clues in the problems.

Selected Answers

Problem 1

The Phrase	Using Arithmetic	Using an Algebra Expression
Pick any number.		n
Multiply by three.		$3n$
Add four.		$3n + 4$
Subtract one.		$3n + 3$
Divide by three.		$n + 1$
Subtract the number you started with.		1
Your answer is one.		1

Problem 2

The Phrase	Using Arithmetic	Using an Algebra Expression
Pick any number.		n
Add four.		$n + 4$
Multiply by two.		$2(n + 4) = 2n + 8$
Subtract the number you started with.		$n + 8$
Subtract eight.		n
This is the number you started with.		n

Variation

Students can be given the algebra expressions and asked to write the word clues. For example,

Algebra Expression	Word Clues
n	
$n + 5$	
$2(n + 5) = 2n + 10$	
$2n$	
$\frac{1}{2}(2n) = n$	
n	

Writing in Math

Journal questions:

1. Write a Mind Reading or Algebra? problem that has at least four verbal clues. Then solve it by substituting a number for the variables in your problem.

2. Explain how the Mind Reading or Algebra? problems help demonstrate why algebra is called *generalized arithmetic.*

Mind Reading or Algebra?

Name _____

Date _____ Class _____

Directions: Learn how algebra can help you *become a "mind reader."* In each of these problems, read the algebraic expressions in the first column. Follow the directions, assign a number, and solve the arithmetic problem. Then substitute an algebraic expression for each of the numbers. Be sure that the solution to each algebra expression is the same as the number you get using arithmetic. Some clues have been provided.

Problem 1

The Phrase	*Using Arithmetic*	*Using an Algebra Expression*
Pick any number		n
Multiply by 3		
Add 4		$3n + 4$
Subtract 1		
Divide by 3		
Subtract the number you started with		
Your answer is 1		

Problem 2

The Phrase	*Using Arithmetic*	*Using an Algebra Expression*
Pick any number		n
Add 4		
Multiply by 2		$2(n + 4) = 2n + 8$
Subtract the number you started with		
Subtract 8		
This is the number you started with		

Mind Reading or
Algebra?—Make Up Your Own

Name _____

Date _____ Class _____

Directions: Work with your partner to make up an original Mind Reading or Algebra? puzzle. As you design your puzzle, first write out the word phrase and the algebra expression. Fill in the numbers using arithmetic. *When you are sure that all of your clues are correct, copy only the phrases in the second table.* You will share the second puzzle with other groups.

The Phrase	Using Arithmetic	Using an Algebra Expression

The Phrase	Using Arithmetic	Using an Algebra Expression

Geometry 3
Our Mathematical Window to the World

Geometry 3

Our Mathematical Window to the World

Where there is matter, there is geometry.

—Johannes Kepler

Geometry is the mathematics of shape and form. It is one way we can relate school mathematics to our physical world. The NCTM's Standards (2000) state that the study of the geometry of one, two, and three dimensions should (1) help develop spatial sense, (2) encourage students to use geometric models to represent and solve problems, and (3) provide opportunities for students to explore transformations and use symmetry to analyze mathematical relationships. We can use three-dimensional models (such as blocks, balls, and cylinders) and two-dimensional models (such as geoboards, drawings, and graph paper) to develop geometry concepts and help students recognize and differentiate between shapes.

The van Hieles' research (as cited in Fuys, Geddes, and Tischler 1988) indicates that geometric knowledge progresses through a hierarchy of levels. Children first learn how to recognize an entire shape and then progress to analyzing the relevant properties of that shape. Only after they become proficient with this can they progress to seeing the relationship between different shapes, their similarities and differences.

The activities presented in this chapter give students experiences with hands-on activities that help them identify, describe, and classify geometric shapes and develop a formal understanding, while experiencing their physical qualities. By folding, measuring, and building geometric models, students empirically discover the properties or rules of a class of both two- and three-dimensional shapes.

The geometry activities in this chapter focus on the relationships between squares and cubes. They are designed to enhance spatial visualization and reasoning and allow students the opportunity to explore other avenues and approaches to learning mathematics.

FOLDING A TANGRAM

The Folding a Tangram activity connects fractions and geometry in a way that has built-in appeal to students. It allows them to experience the size of each shape, both spatially and symbolically, and encourages them to follow oral directions.

Tangram Thinkers, a problem-solving activity, permits students to use their newly created tangram pieces to construct polygons. By working in pairs, students develop their interpersonal intelligence while solving a problem that nourishes their visual-spatial intelligence.

MAKING A TANGRAM QUILT

The Making a Tangram Quilt project uses the tangram pieces produced in the Folding a Tangram activity to design quilt squares that will eventually become a part of a class quilt. Each student begins by designing his or her own tangram quilt square and analyzing it to compute the fractional part of the whole each color represents. The fraction is then converted to a percentage. Students, now working in pairs, choose the design they like best and problem solve how to transfer the design to paper or cloth; this square represents their contribution to the class quilt. This project takes students through the real-life process of producing a quilt—from creating the pieces to designing the squares, and finally, to creating the quilt. What begins as a simple fraction activity becomes a work of art.

PENTOMINOES

Pentominoes is an informal activity that invites students to use the vocabulary of geometry in a dynamic way while enhancing their visual-spatial intelligence. Students find all the combinations of five tiles that touch side to side. They experience the transformations of rotation and reflection while they problem-solve solutions.

OPEN-TOP BOXES

The Open-Top Boxes activity has relevance from fifth-grade math through calculus. Using scissors and tape, students build and compute the volume of each open-topped box to find the one with the greatest area. While the solution can be found using abstract symbols and formulas, it is possible to approximate a solution by trial and testing.

EXPLORATIONS WITH CEREAL BOXES

Explorations With Cereal Boxes uses a commonly found household item to explore some difficult geometric concepts. Students use rectangular prisms and three-dimensional figures, measure the lengths of the sides, and compute both the surface area and volume. How surprising to find the area (a two-dimensional concept) of a three-dimensional shape! Following this, students explore the cost and nutritional value of cereal. Be sure to keep the cereal boxes because this activity precedes the building of a cereal box from a flat piece of tagboard. Can this be done?

THE PAINTED CUBE

If you build a $3 \times 3 \times 3$ inch cube and throw it into a bucket of paint, you have "The Painted Cube." Will all of the faces be covered with paint or will some of them be left unpainted? Using cubes and their spatial imaginations, students look for mathematical patterns to make conjectures.

CUBES THAT GROW

Cubes That Grow is another activity that examines both the two-dimensional and three-dimensional qualities of cubes. By exploring the ratio of surface area to volume, students are led to a fascinating discovery. Work along with them to experience it yourself!

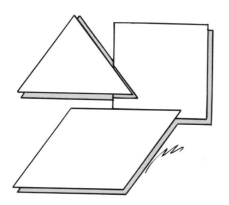

FOLDING A TANGRAM

TEACHER'S PLANNING INFORMATION

Math Topics

Informal geometry, oral directions, mathematical connections

Active Learning

Students will

1. Follow oral directions to fold a paper tangram

2. Use their tangram pieces to visualize shapes and areas of polygons

3. Informally understand geometric terms and the attributes of shapes

4. Use their tangram pieces to solve problems and design a quilt square

Materials

One sheet of 8 1/2 x 11-inch paper; scissors, Folding a Tangram Worksheets (including Tangram Thinkers) for each student

Suggestions for Instruction

Because this exercise requires students to follow oral directions, it is a good idea to demonstrate the folds while students have a copy of the written directions in front of them. In this way, students can see and hear the directions at the same time.

Give each student a sheet of paper and a pair of scissors. As you give directions and demonstrate, focus on the following:

1. The names of the polygons formed: when folding, isosceles right triangles, right trapezoids, squares, and parallelograms are formed

2. The areas of each of the shapes, if the original square equals 1

3. Which of the polygons are congruent; which are similar (the right triangles are similar)

4. The attributes of each polygon

5. The difference between congruence and similarity

6. What fractional part each tangram piece is of the whole square

Tangram Thinkers, an extension that follows the folding activity, asks students to work in pairs and use their tangram pieces to solve puzzles that develop visual-spatial intelligence.

The Internet has a great many very interesting interactive tangram sites. These are just a few:

- http://pbskids.org/sagwa/games/tangrams/index.html has both easy and difficult puzzles. Students drag the pieces on to the puzzle to try to make the picture shown. For those who need it, hints are offered.

- http://pbskids.org/cyberchase/games/area/tangram.html is another interactive site that offers many different pictures. It is easy for students to rotate the pieces (either clockwise or counterclockwise) to fit them into the designs.

Selected Answers

Answers will vary.

Variation

Students can find the perimeter of triangles using the Pythagorean theorem.

Writing in Math

Journal questions:

1. Describe the attributes of each of the polygons formed when paper folding a tangram.

2. Some of the triangles folded in the tangram activity were similar to each other and some were congruent. Explain the difference between similarity and congruence.

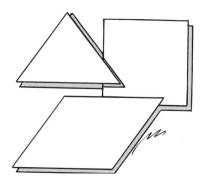

Folding a Tangram

Direction Sheet

Directions: Listen to and watch your teacher's demonstration. You can also follow along reading these written directions.

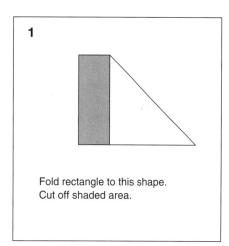

1

Fold rectangle to this shape.
Cut off shaded area.

2

Open the paper. Now there are two triangles.

1. What kind of triangles are they?

2. If the area of the square is one unit, what is the area of each triangle?

3

A   E   B

M

F

C

Cut the triangles apart. Use one of the large triangles for these pieces.

Fold on dotted line by bringing point B to point M. Cut off the triangle (BEF).

1. What is the area of triangle ABC?

2. What is the name of the polygon (AEFC)?

4

E   B

F

You now have:

Triangle EBF, which is the medium-sized triangle of your set of tangrams.

Cut out the triangle EBF. Set this triangle aside.

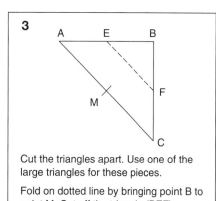
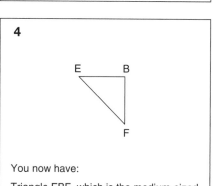

5

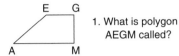

Fold point F onto point E.

1. What is polygon AEGM called?

Fold point C onto point M. Cut at lines FH and GM. You have now formed two more polygons. What are they?

6

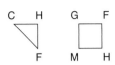

You now have:

Triangle FHC, which is one of the small triangles, and GFHM which is the square of your tangram. Set these pieces aside.

7

Fold point M to point E.

You have now formed triangle GMK and parallelogram AEGK. Cut apart the triangle and parallelogram.

8

GMK is the second small triangle.

AEGK is the parallelogram.

9

Take the other half of the square (the other large triangle) and fold it in half. Now, cut the triangle on the fold.

You have the last two pieces of the tangram.

10

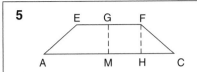

A TANGRAM

2 Large Triangles
1 Medium Triangle
2 Small Triangles
1 Square
1 Parallelogram

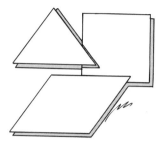

Tangram Thinkers

Worksheet

Name _____

Date _____ Class _____

Directions: Work with a partner and use your tangram pieces to see how many different ways, if any, you can form these polygons. You can describe your combinations of pieces you use by using the numbers assigned to each in the diagram. For this activity, consider the square (a special rectangle) as a unique figure.

Can you form each polygon using these numbers of pieces?	Square	Rectangle	Triangle	Trapezoid	Parallelogram
1					
2					
3					
4					
5					
6					
7					

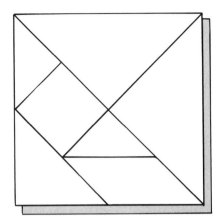

MAKING A TANGRAM QUILT

TEACHER'S PLANNING INFORMATION

Suggestions for Instruction

Discuss with the students how they should go about designing, in pairs, a square using their tangram pieces. It is important they understand that they should not plan to use all seven pieces and may reuse shapes to complete a pleasant design. For example, a quilt square could be made with only small triangles and squares or with the two large triangles and combinations of small triangles and parallelograms. There is a great deal of mathematics in this lesson! For students to design a quilt square with no overlapping pieces and no gaps, the pieces or parts of the square must add up to 64/64, 1, or 100%.

A paper quilt can be made by forming a rectangular array of the squares produced by the pairs of students. A 3 square by 4 square quilt represents 12 pairs or 24 students; a 4 square by 5 square quilt represents 20 pairs or 40 students.

If you decide to make a fabric quilt, designs must be drawn with fabric crayons, following the directions on the crayon box. (You can find the nearest location selling fabric crayons by calling 1–800-CRAYOLA.) Cut the fabric with ¼-inch seam allowance on each side of the square to allow sewing.

You can design your quilt in a number of ways. Here is an example of an interesting quilt design:

Remember: To sew, pieces need 1/4-inch seam allowance on each side.

Quilts are very geometric and have many applications in the math classroom. They can be used to focus on symmetry, fractions, geometric shapes, and tiling (tessellations). One Web site, http://teacher.scholastic.com/products/instructor/Jan04_quiltmath.htm,

Math Topics

Geometry, fractions, decimals, percentages, problem solving, connections

Active Learning

Students will

1. Use tangram pieces to design a quilt square with a partner

2. Problem solve a means to copy their design to an 8 x 8 grid that is a different size than the original

3. Calculate the number, fractional part, and percentage of each color used in their designs as it relates to the entire or whole square

4. Transfer the design representing the best work of the pair to an 8 × 8 grid

Materials

Tangram pieces from the tangram activity; copies of Making a Tangram Quilt worksheets 1 and 2; crayons, colored pencils, or markers; an 8 × 8 grid for students to transpose their designs (this can be used as the final design if you are going to make a paper quilt. Note: To make grids that are 8 × 8 inches, cut them from a roll of 1-inch grid paper); fabric crayons for designing the actual quilt square (if you do not intend to make a fabric quilt, these are not necessary)

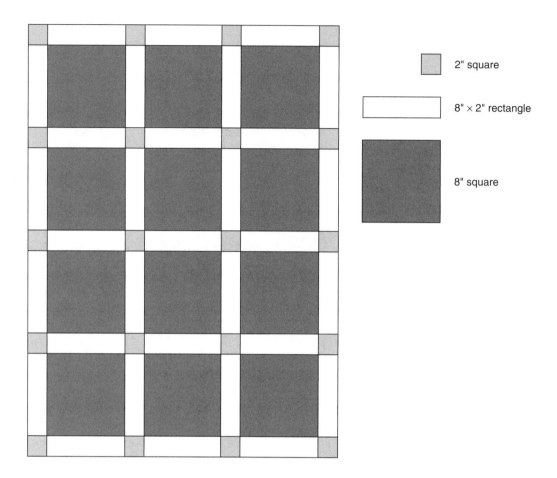

▨	2" square
▭	8" × 2" rectangle
▮	8" square

has interesting suggestions about how mathematics teachers can make connections with a quilting unit. A Quilt Math reproducible sheet can be downloaded and used to introduce or revisit a variety of skills.

A beautiful and extensive Web site with too many options to name is http://www.aghines.com/Quilt/Lessonplans/lessonplans.htm. But some links give students the opportunity to color in unbelievable quilt patterns, design their own quilts (this is interactive) and use lights and darks to create quilt designs. The site is designed to give teachers ideas as well as provide links for student use.

Selected Answers

The numbers of squares, fractions, and decimals will vary on students' Worksheet 2, but the number of squares should equal 64; the fraction 64/64 or 1; the percent 100%.

Variation

While this activity works well as designed, it is also possible for students to actually sew a quilt using fabric. If this is done, students need to do the following:

1. Cut out pieces of an 8×8 grid.

2. Make pattern pieces to cut the fabric (these need a 1/4-inch seam allowance cut on each edge of the pattern piece).

3. Measure a 1/4-inch seam line and carefully sew on this line.

Writing in Math

Journal questions:

1. What fractional part of your tangram is the large triangle? The medium triangle? The small triangle? The square? The parallelogram? Explain your answer.

2. Which of your tangram pieces have the same area? The same perimeter? Explain your answer.

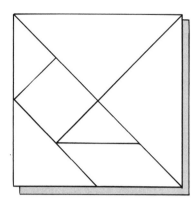

Making a Tangram Quilt

The 8 x 8 Grid

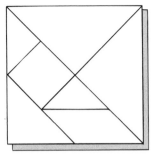

Making a Tangram Quilt

Worksheet

Name _____

Date _____ Class _____

Directions: After you have designed a quilt square with your tangram pieces, copy the design onto the 8 × 8 grid. You will need to analyze the design and copy it carefully. Be sure that each section is colored in (any spaces will be holes in your quilt) and that no pieces overlap (these will cause bulges). Each person must design his or her own quilt square and complete the table. Explain what fractional part of the quilt square each color represents.

Color	Number of Squares	Fraction of the Square	Percentage of the Square
Totals			

Describe (1) how you calculated the fractional part of the quilt each color represented and (2) how you converted that fraction to a percent.

_____

_____

What are all of the totals equivalent to? _____

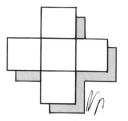

PENTOMINOES

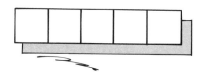

TEACHER'S PLANNING INFORMATION

Math Topics

Geometry, measurement, problem solving, area, perimeter

Active Learning

Students will

1. Use a grid to find the 12 different pentomino pieces

2. Use their pentominoes to solve area problems

3. Experiment with transformations to eliminate duplicate pentominoes

4. Work collaboratively to problem solve the solutions

Materials

Pentominoes worksheets; scissors; markers or colored pencils

Suggestions for Instruction

Polyominoes are geometric shapes that are formed by combining squares. For example, monominoes are made of one square, dominoes are formed from two squares, triominoes from three squares, tetrominoes from four, pentominoes from five, hexominoes from six, and so on. This table lists the number of unique arrangements for up to six squares:

Students will be problem solving to find the 12 different pentominoes that can be formed. There are many interesting Web sites that focus on polyominoes in general and pentominoes in particular. One that has fascinating information about different polyominoes is http://www.recmath.com/PolyPages. Others are interactive sites that allow students to try to form the 6×10 rectangle that is one of the three puzzles on worksheet 2. On http://www.math.clemson.edu/~rsimms/java/pentominoes/index2.html, students can move, rotate, flip, and more to complete a 6×10 pentomino jigsaw puzzle.

In the math classroom, place students into working pairs and give each pair a copy of the Pentominoes worksheet.

Number of Squares	1	2	3	4	5	6
Number of Arrangements	1	1	2	5	12	35

Discuss what *legal* and *illegal* pentominoes are, and show examples of each. Legal pentominoes have a side touching; they are not merely joined at a point:

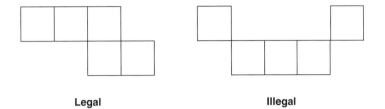

Legal   **Illegal**

There are 12 different and unique pentominoes. (Students should not be given this information—it is important that they problem solve and experiment to find them.)  Caution the students about rotations and flips. If a pentomino can be rotated or reflected and look like another, it is not a different pentomino. It is the same one! Here's an example:

When the students are finished, ask them the following questions:

1. Do all of these pentominoes have the same area?

2. Do they have the same perimeter? Which has the largest perimeter? Which has the smallest?

Selected Answers

The 12 pentominoes are shown in the following figure.

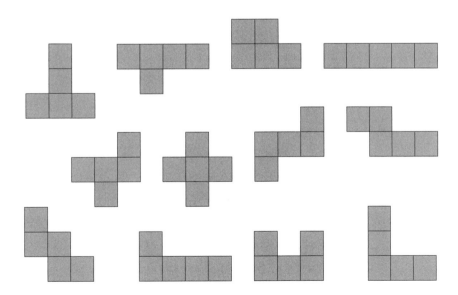

Worksheet 2, Jigsaw Puzzles, asks students to form three different-sized rectangles using their tangram pieces. As discussed earlier, there are multiple solutions to these puzzles. The 4×15 puzzle has 368 different solutions, the 5×12 puzzle has 1, 010 solutions, and the 6×10 has over 2,000 different solutions!

Variation

This is an extension activity that is quite challenging. Since there are 35 hexominoes, give students centimeter graph paper and encourage them to find all of the possible hexominoes.

Writing in Math

Journal questions:

1. Which of the pentominoes can be folded to form an open box? Explain your answer with diagrams.

2. Do any of the pentominoes display symmetry? Explain your answer with diagrams.

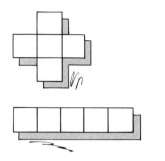

Pentominoes

Worksheet 1

Problem: Arrange five squares into different shapes, following the rule that edges must always be completely touching. Find all 12 possible solutions. Be careful that you do not have congruent shapes that have only been rotated or reflected. Record your solutions on the grid paper lightly with pencil. When you are sure that you have all of the pentominoes, use colored pencils to make them easier to see. These pieces will be cut out and used to solve the Pentomino Jigsaw Puzzles.

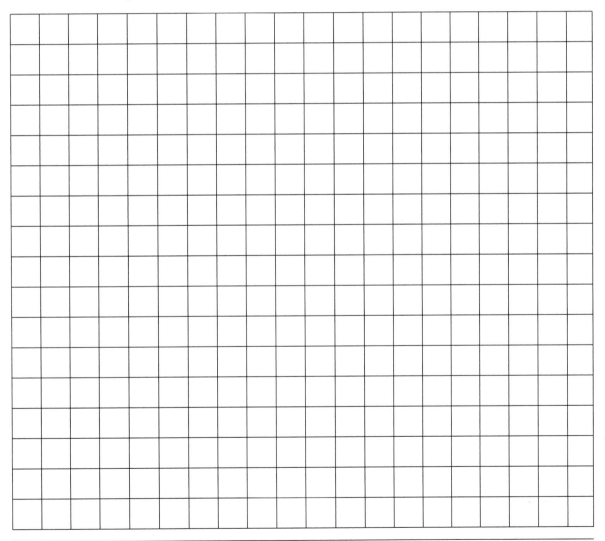

Pentominoes

Worksheet 2: Jigsaw Puzzles

Name _____

Date _____ Class _____

Use your 12 pentominoes and the specially designed grids to form the following:

1. A 6×10 rectangle

2. A 5×12 rectangle

3. A 4×15 rectangle

Record and color in your solutions in the appropriate grid. Use different colors to separate your pentomino pieces so each piece can be identified. You may want to color in both sides of your pentomino piece as sometimes the piece must be turned over or around to fit into the puzzle.

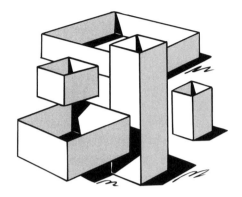

OPEN-TOP BOXES

TEACHER'S PLANNING INFORMATION

Suggestions for Instruction

Use a 17×17 centimeter (cm) grid cutout as a sample to demonstrate how an open-topped box can be formed by cutting a square out of each corner and folding up the sides. The area of the base is now 15×15, or 225 square units. To find the volume, multiply the area of the base, 225, by the height, 1. The volume of this box is 225 cubic units. Explain to the students that they will be working to find the box with the greatest volume by decreasing the area of the base and increasing the height. What happens to the volume?

Have students work in pairs. When students have completed the experiment, discuss the results. Encourage students to experiment by substituting numbers other than whole numbers for the height to see how close they can get to the box with the biggest volume.

Selected Answers

When the base of the box is 15 cm $\times$ 15 cm and the height is 5 cm, the volume is 1,125 cm³. When the base of the box is 13 cm $\times$ 13 cm and the height is 6 cm, the volume is 1,014 cm³. So the box with the greatest volume has sides between 13 and 15 cm and a height between 5 and 6 cm.

Math Topics

Geometry, data collection, spatial reasoning, problem solving, computation

Active Learning

Students will

1. Work collaboratively to problem solve

2. Find the open-top box with the greatest volume

3. Use problem-solving strategies to approach the desired solution

4. Collect and organize data in a table

5. Compute the volume of a rectangular prism

Materials

Open-Top Boxes worksheets, scissors, tape, calculators

Variation

Have students find the volumes of boxes with original bases of 15, 16, 18, and 19 and record their findings on the same table to discover if there is a pattern.

Writing in Math

Journal questions:

1. Explain how you found the box with the greatest volume.

2. How do you account for the fact that the box that had the greatest area on its base did not have the greatest volume?

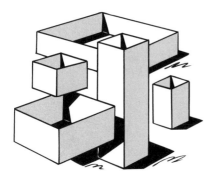

Open-Top Boxes

Worksheet I

Name _____

Date _____ Class _____

Directions: The 17×17 grid on the next page can be made into an open-topped box by cutting squares from each of the four corners and folding up the sides. The volume of a box is found by multiplying the area of its base by its height. Work with your partner to form an open-ended box with the greatest volume, but keep the base a square. Use the following table to find a pattern that might help you solve this problem.

Length of Base	Width of Base	Height of Box	Volume of Box

The dimensions of the box with the greatest volume are: _____

On the back of this page, describe how you solved this problem.

Open-Top Boxes

17 cm × 17 cm Grid

EXPLORATIONS WITH CEREAL BOXES

TEACHER'S PLANNING INFORMATION

Math Topics

Measurement, solid geometry, surface area, volume, computation

Active Learning

Students will

1. Analyze the sides of a cereal box (rectangular prism) to find the area of each surface

2. Compute the volume of a rectangular prism

3. Compute whether the box with the largest volume has the greatest weight

4. Compute the cost per ounce (or gram) for each cereal

5. Work collaboratively to make real-world connections

Materials

Cereal boxes, calculators, rulers, Explorations With Cereal Boxes worksheets

Suggestions for Instruction

Hold up a cereal box and ask these questions:

- What is the difference between the surface area and the volume of this box?
- What information would we need to find each?
- Why would we need to know the surface area of an object? Would knowing the surface area help us figure out how much wrapping paper we need to wrap a gift?

Explain why we might need to know the volume of a box.

Students generally have a very poor understanding of these two concepts. The exercises in this book are two-dimensional problems that require a three-dimensional solution. To find the surface area, the box can be dissected in the following manner:

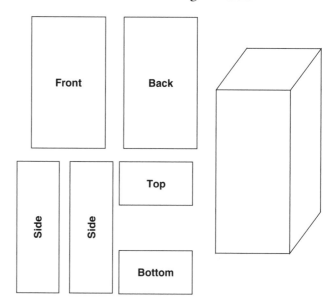

The volume is found by finding the area of the bottom (the base) and multiplying it by the height of the box. By using the box as a manipulative, students can experience the size and measurements required. It is best if students work in groups of three or four.

Selected Answers

Answers will vary.

Variation

Students can find the surface area and volume of other polyhedra. When finding the area of pyramids, students are given practice finding the area of triangles.

Writing in Math

Journal questions:

1. Explain what you did to find the surface area of your cereal box. How did it differ from finding the volume?

2. When finding the price per ounce of various cereals, which was the most expensive? Was it the healthiest? Were sugar-coated cereals more expensive than the others? Discuss what you found out about the way cereals are priced.

Explorations With Cereal Boxes

Worksheet 1

Name _____

Date _____ Class _____

Directions: Find five cereal boxes that are different sizes and measure the lengths of the sides to find the surface area of each of the boxes. When you have found the surface area of each box, find its volume and write it in the appropriate space below.

Name of Cereal	Surface Area of						Total Surface Area
	Top	Bottom	Front	Back	Side	Side	

Name of Cereal	Volume

Explorations With Cereal Boxes

Worksheet 2

Name _____

Date _____ Class _____

Have you ever wondered which was the best buy in cereals? Is it always the one in the biggest box or the one that costs the least? Now that you've found the surface area and volume of some of these cereal boxes, let's look at what's inside the box—the cereal! Choose eight different cereals and use the table below to list them, figure out their price per ounce, their price per pound, the number of grams of sugar per ounce and per pound, and rank them from 1 to 8, based on the cost (1 is the most expensive; 8 is the least expensive).

Name of Cereal	Price per oz	Price per lb	Grams of Sugar per oz	Grams of Sugar per lb	Rank 1 – 8

Which cereal do you consider the healthiest? Why? _____

_____

Is it the best buy? How do you explain this? Write your answer on the back of this page.

THE PAINTED CUBE

TEACHER'S PLANNING INFORMATION

Math Topics

Geometry, problem solving, data collection, and analysis

Active Learning

Students will

1. Problem solve the number of faces that would be "painted" if a $3 \times 3 \times 3$ cube were dropped into a bucket of paint

2. Record their data in a table

3. Analyze the data to describe a pattern

Materials

The Painted Cube worksheet, calculators, 27 cubes for pairs of students to use as manipulatives, if possible

Suggestions for Instruction

Hold up one cube and ask students, "If this cube were thrown into a bucket of red paint, how many faces would be painted red?" Put together a $2 \times 2 \times 2$ cube so students have a smaller visual model to work from. Go through the questions in the table and discuss the answers with the students. There are relationships between the number of painted faces and the edges, vertices, and faces of the cube. By discovering these patterns, students are able to predict the results of a painted $n \times n \times n$ cube.

An interactive activity that allows students to view a three-dimensional shape from the front, side, and top and then discusses the surface area and volume of the shape can be found at http://www.shodor.org/inter activate/activities/sa_volume/index.html. Extensive teacher's pages accompany all of the activities on this interactivate Web site.

Selected Answers

There are no cubes that are painted on all of the faces; the three painted faces are always the corners—eight on a cube; those with two faces painted occur on the edges between the corners; cubes with one face painted occur as squares on the six faces of the original cube. The cubes with no faces painted are the cubes inside the surface.

Variation

The problem can be extended to have students find the volume of each of the cubes as they grow. This problem assumes each cube has a side of 1 cm. For example, one cube has a volume of 1 cm^3, a $2 \times 2 \times 2$ cube has a volume of 8 cm^3, and so on.

Writing in Math

Journal question:

1. Discuss the relationship between the number of faces of the cube that are "painted" and the vertices, faces, and edges of the cube.

The Painted Cube

Worksheet

Name _____

Date _____ Class _____

You have a cube like the one shown at the right, but it has been thrown into a bucket of red paint. The outside is all red, but the inside is not. Compete the following table and see if you and your partner see a pattern developing. It will help you answer the questions at the end of the activity.

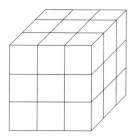

Size of Cube	Number of Painted Faces			
	0	1	2	3
$2 \times 2 \times 2$				
$3 \times 3 \times 3$				
$4 \times 4 \times 4$				
$5 \times 5 \times 5$				
$6 \times 6 \times 6$				
$n \times n \times n$				

Discuss the data you collected with your partner and describe the pattern that you see.

_____

_____

_____

_____

CUBES THAT GROW

TEACHER'S PLANNING INFORMATION

Suggestions for Instruction

Students work with partners to find the relationship between the surface area and volume of cubes. For a $2 \times 2 \times 2$ cube, the surface area is $4 \times 6 = 24$. (The number of squares on each side is four, and there are six faces.) The volume, however, is $2^3 = 8$. An interesting pattern develops as the area of the base increases because the constant we use to find the surface area is always the area of the base multiplied by 6.

Ask students, "Do you think that the volume of the cube will ever be equal to the surface area? Do you think that the volume will ever be greater than the surface area?" A good discussion will help establish how well each of the students understands the underlying concepts of volume and surface area.

Variation

Using cubes, students can construct rectangular prisms and problem solve the relationship between surface area and volume of this polyhedron.

Writing in Math

Journal questions:

1. At what point is the ratio of surface area to volume equal to 1? When is it less than 1? More than 1? Explain your answers.

2. How can you explain the rapid growth of volume and the slower growth of surface area?

Math Topics

Geometry, spatial reasoning, patterns, computation, problem solving, data collection, analysis

Active Learning

Students will

1. Use cubes to problem solve the relationship between surface area and volume

2. Use collected data to define this relationship for a cube with a side of n units

3. Use formulas to find surface area and volume

Materials

Cubes (at least 27 for each pair of students), Cubes That Grow worksheets, calculators

Selected Answers

Edge	1	2	3	4	5	6	n
Area of Base	1	4	9	16	25	36	n^2
Surface Area	6	24	54	96	150	216	$6n$
Volume	1	8	27	64	125	216	n^3
$\dfrac{\text{Surface Area}}{\text{Volume}}$	$6/1 = 6$	$24/8 = 3$	$54/27 = 2$	$96/64 = 1.5$	$150/125 = 1.2$	$216/216 = 1$	$6n/n^3$

Cubes That Grow

Worksheet

Name _____

Date _____ Class _____

With identically sized cubes, work with your partner to construct cubes with edges of 1, 2, 3, and possibly 4. Enter your data in the following table to find a pattern that can be applied to a cube with "n" number of sides.

Edge	1	2	3	4	5	6	n
Area of Base	1						
Surface Area	6						
Volume	1						
Surface Area / Volume	$\frac{6}{1} = 6$						

What pattern do you observe? _____

Why do you think this occurs? (Be sure to consider the formulas used to find surface area and volume.)

_____

_____

_____

_____

The Measure of Mathematics 4

The Measure of Mathematics 4

The trouble with measurement is its seeming simplicity.

—Anonymous

In the so-called real world, we use measurements to answer questions such as "How big is it?", "How long is it?", "How much time does it take?", or "How much does it weigh?" Two more related questions are "Is an exact number needed?" and "Would an estimate be accurate enough?" To answer these questions, students need hands-on experiences that permit them to explore the world around them.

The measures of mathematics consist of more than just measurements of length. Students must understand the concepts of time, weight, and mass.

Among the recommendations of the NCTM (2000) in *Principles and Standards for School Mathematics* are that students understand (1) both customary and metric units, (2) how these units relate to one another and how to convert within the same system, (3) how to select appropriate units of measurement, and (4) how to solve problems related to scale factors using ratio and proportion. The activities in this chapter are practical applications of the NCTM's recommendations while providing motivating and active learning experiences for today's students.

JUST HOW BIG IS THE STATUE OF LIBERTY?

On Bedloe's Island in New York Bay is one of our country's treasures. It's called the Statue of Liberty. It's the statue of a beautiful woman, and it rises more than 306 feet from the bottom of her pedestal to the tip of her torch. Could you figure out how big the Statue of Liberty is if you knew that her arm is 42 feet long? This is the question posed to your students. By taking their own measurements and using scale factors and ratio and proportion, students are able to find the size of Lady Liberty. Last, by designing a scale drawing, they will have approached this problem using their artistic creativity and mathematics!

GUMMI WORMS

Edible worms? What's this world coming to? The Gummi Worms activity tempts your students to describe the physical attributes of Gummi Worms: what they look like; the fractional part of each of the colors; how much elasticity they have. By measuring and describing their worms, students are engaging in a rather unconventional view of math.

WHAT HAPPENED 1,000,000 SECONDS AGO?

What happened 1,000,000 seconds ago? What's wrong with this question? It's almost as confusing as asking, "How many feet is it from Los Angeles to New York?" We're dealing with extremely inappropriate units of measurement. By converting to appropriate units, your students will discover some interesting facts.

HOW LONG WOULD IT TAKE TO WALK TO CHINA—THROUGH THE CENTER OF THE EARTH?

Did anyone ever tell you that if you dug a deep enough hole, you would end up in China? What they meant was, if you were to dig through the center of the Earth—on the diameter—you would end up on the other side of the globe. That's probably true, but you would be in the Indian Ocean if you started out in the United States. How Long Would It Take to Walk to China? requires students, working in groups, to find each member's rate of speed by using the formula $R = \frac{D}{T}$. Then using the group average, they calculate how long it would take to walk the Earth's diameter. This activity gives students the opportunity to problem solve using metric units of measurement and mathematical formulas.

HEIGHT VERSUS SHOE LENGTH

We, as humans, look somewhat alike because we are proportional. It is possible to develop mathematical constants when comparing the relationship, or ratio, between various body measurements. Artists have been using these ratios for centuries to produce what is considered art. Height Versus Shoe Length has students actively involved in taking measurements and collecting data to discover if there is a relationship between the size of one's shoe and one's height. While there are some exceptions, generally speaking, the taller a person is, the larger the shoe size. This relationship, or correlation, is explored when the data is graphed on a scatterplot and the coordinates on the graph are analyzed to see the "shape" of the data.

EGGSCETERA

Does it pay to buy jumbo rather than large eggs? Are we getting a better buy because of the larger size? EggsCetera is an activity where students measure the circumference, mass, and height of different-sized eggs and use their data to compute the best buy.

All of the activities in this chapter provide *active* experiences to help students understand the concepts involved with measurement while they are involved in hands-on projects.

JUST HOW BIG IS THE STATUE OF LIBERTY?

TEACHER'S PLANNING INFORMATION

Math Topics

Measurement, estimation, ratio, proportion, data collection, analysis, scale drawing, computation

Active Learning

Students will

1. Estimate the size of the Statue of Liberty by using ratio and proportion

2. Make suppositions based on data collection and analysis

3. Use ratio and proportion to problem solve

4. Work in cooperative groups to problem solve

Materials

Just How Big Is the Statue of Liberty? Worksheets 1–3; tape measures, yard sticks, and 12-inch rulers; calculators; graph paper

Suggestions for Instruction

Discuss with students the length of the statue's arm. Take some haphazard measurements and try to estimate how many times larger than life the Statue of Liberty really is.

Place students in groups of four, read the directions on Worksheet 1, and have students complete the data collection by carefully measuring their own body parts. Group averages supply an average decimal ratio, and using ratio and proportion, students calculate the size of various body parts on the Statue of Liberty.

On the next page are some of the actual measurements of the Statue of Liberty. Additional measurements are given to help students with their scale drawings. A copy of this can be made and shared with students when scale drawings are being made.

After all of the groups have completed their own data collection and computation, the last phase of the project is the scale drawing of the statue. Graph paper of ¼ inch is supplied. Students must determine the appropriate scale, design their scale drawings, and create their works of art.

The Statue of Liberty is a National Park and has an official Web site: http://www.nps.gov/stli/

Another site that is loaded with both historical information about the statue and its dimensions (including weight) is http://www.endex.com/gf/buildings/liberty/libertyfacts.htm.

Used in Activity (*)	Body Part	Height (in feet and inches)
*	Height from base to torch	151 ft. 1 in.
	Foundation of pedestal to torch	305 ft. 1 in.
*	Height from foot to top of head	111 ft. 1 in.
*	Length of hand	16 ft. 5 in.
*	Length of head	17 ft. 3 in.
*	Width of head (from ear to ear)	10 ft. 0 in.
*	Length of neck	10 ft. 9 in.
	Length of eye (from side to side)	2 ft. 6 in.
	Length of nose	4 ft. 6 in.
	Right arm length	42 ft. 0 in.
	Thickness of waist	35 ft. 0 in.
	Width of mouth	3 ft. 0 in.

SOURCE: National Park Service, U.S. Department of the Interior: http://www.nps.gov/stli/prod02.htm

Selected Answers

While answers will vary, let's assume that the average height of a student is 5 feet 6 inches. The height of the Statue of Liberty from her foot to the top of her head is approximately 111 feet. Using the ratio $\frac{\text{Statue of Liberty Measurement}}{\text{Student Measurement}}$ or $\frac{111}{5.5} \approx 20$, the statue is about 20 times larger than the average student. The ratios obtained by students will depend on their actual measurements.

Variation

Jonathan Swift's *Gulliver's Travels* has an interesting section describing Gulliver's adventures in Lilliput. There are many references to the relative size of Gulliver and the little people. This would make an interesting extension to Lady Liberty.

Writing in Math

Journal questions:

1. How can ratio and proportion be helpful in estimating the size of large objects?

2. Describe an activity that could be made easier by using ratio and proportion.

Just How Big Is the Statue of Liberty?

Worksheet 1

Name _____

Date _____ Class _____

The Statue of Liberty, on Bedloe's Island in New York Bay, is one of the largest statues in the world. Lady Liberty rises about 305 feet from the bottom of her pedestal to the tip of her torch. Designed by Frédéric Auguste Bartholdi, the Statue of Liberty was a gift to the people of the United States from the people of France. Lady Liberty is a very large woman. The length of her right arm is 42 feet! Your group's job is to figure out her remaining dimensions by using your own measurements and ratio and proportion.

Directions: Find the length of the right arm of each member of your group. Then find the average length of the arms. By setting up a ratio, you can compute how many times larger the statue's arm is than your group's average. Then take the other measurements asked for in this activity. Use this arm ratio you calculated to calculate the size of the rest of the statue. To find the ratio of the size of the Statue of Liberty's arm to the size of a student's arm, use this equation: $\dfrac{42 \text{ feet}}{\text{Group average (in feet)}} =$

Group Member	Length of Arm	Length of Hand	Height (from heel to top of head)	Width of Head	Length of Head	Length of Neck
Average						

Round the decimal ratio to the nearest 1/100 and use that to estimate the body part lengths of the statue.

Just How Big Is the Statue of Liberty?

Worksheet 2

Name _____

Date _____ Class _____

Directions: Use the data you collected to estimate the sizes of the listed parts of the Statue of Liberty. When all of the groups have finished, your teacher will give you the actual measurements. Enter those in the fourth column. You are asked to compare your estimated measurements with the actual measurements and find the percentage of error: $\frac{\text{Estimated} - \text{Actual}}{\text{Actual}} \times 100 = \text{Percent of Error}$. Enter the percentage of error in Column 5.

1	2	3	4	5
Average Length of	*The Group's Measurements*	*Estimated Statue of Liberty Measurements*	*Actual Measurements*	*Percentage of Error (computed vs. actual)*
Arm				
Hand				
Height				
Width of Head				
Length of Head				
Length of Neck				

How many times larger than life is the Statue of Liberty? Explain. _____

_____

How would you describe the accuracy of this activity in estimating the measurements of the Statue of Liberty? What do you think contributed to its accuracy or inaccuracy? Write your answers on the back of this page.

_____

Just How Big Is the Statue of Liberty?

Worksheet 3

Name _____

Date _____ Class _____

Use this grid to design and draw to scale a picture of the Statue of Liberty. Your teacher has additional measurements not used earlier to help you make a more realistic picture. This is a 1/4-inch grid.

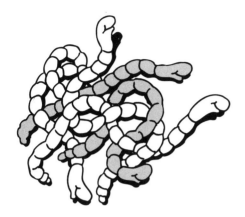

GUMMI WORMS

TEACHER'S PLANNING INFORMATION

Suggestions for Instruction

Hold up a Gummi Worm and ask students to describe its physical attributes. What does it look like? How many different colors does it have? About what fractional part is each color of the whole worm? What percentage?

Students are asked to measure each section of the Gummi Worm and record the length of each section to the nearest millimeter. When the total length is found, students calculate the fractional part of the whole Gummi Worm that each section represents and then convert that to a percentage. It is a surprise that not each section is the same length.

Students then experiment with the concept of elasticity by stretching the Gummi Worm and waiting for it to shrink back again. Although it does shrink, it does not go back to its original size and so has less elasticity than perhaps a rubber band. Students are asked to remeasure the stretched Gummi Worm and calculate the percentage of growth that has taken place. A ratio that can be used to find this percentage is

$$\frac{\text{Stretched length} - \text{Original length}}{\text{Original length}} \times 100 = \% \text{ of growth} \cdot$$

When groups have completed their data collection, ask students to share their data with the rest of the class on the Class Data Chart. The class data can be analyzed to find the mean length of Gummi Worms, what the class's median length was, and if there appears to be a mode.

When all the data are collected, have students graph their data on an overhead transparency. At this point, the class has a variety of representations to help them understand the data.

Math Topics

Measurement, data collection and analysis, fractions, percentages, graphing, mathematical connections

Active Learning

Students will

1. Work collaboratively with a partner

2. Measure to the nearest millimeter

3. Compute the fractional part of the whole

4. Compute the percentage of a whole

5. Calculate percentage of growth

6. Experiment with elasticity

7. Analyze data and graph class results

Materials

One Gummi Worm for each pair of students, metric rulers, copies of Gummi Worms Worksheet 1, calculators, transparency of Gummi Worms Worksheet 2

Selected Answers

Answers will vary.

Variation

While a Gummi Worm is a nonregular polyhedron, it is possible to find its volume (it is an irregular cylinder) and average mass. In addition, it does have some elasticity. Other everyday items could be examined and the property of elasticity investigated.

Another interesting follow-up has built-in motivation—it's a recipe called Dirt With Gummi Worms. It can be found on http://www.cooks.com. It does not require any cooking but unless it's eaten right away, it will require refrigeration.

DIRT WITH GUMMI WORMS

I large package of chocolate instant pudding mix (prepared per package instructions)

I package of Oreo cookies, crushed (they can be put in a baggie and pounded with the math book)

Line a clay flowerpot with aluminum foil. Sprinkle a layer of crushed Oreos on the bottom of the pot. Spoon about 1/2 of the pudding on top. Sprinkle on a second layer of Oreos. Spoon on the other 1/2 of the pudding. Sprinkle the last 1/3 of the Oreos on the top. Place some Gummi Worms 1/2 way into the pudding mixture and a plastic flower in the center of the pot. ENJOY!

Another interesting Web site to investigate if you want to do some nutritional analysis is http://www.brachs.com/products/product.asp?base_code=324#

Writing in Math

Journal questions:

1. Which of the statistics do you think was most helpful in describing the measurement data collected—the mean, the median, or the mode? Explain your answer.

2. Explain why measuring to the nearest millimeter was a more appropriate unit of measure than measuring to the nearest centimeter.

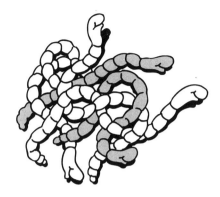

Gummi Worms: An Experiment in Variation

Worksheet 1

Name _____

Date _____ Class _____

Directions: Use your Gummi Worm to do this activity. Measure to the nearest millimeter and record your measurements in the following table.

Describe the colors on your Gummi Worm:

Section	Length of Section	Fractional Part of Section	Percentage of Each Section
1			
2			
3			
4			
Totals			

Now stretch your Gummi Worm as far as it will go, but don't let it break! Now let it go back to its original shape. Remeasure the total length. The new length is _____.

Did it retract to its initial length? Do you believe from this experiment that your Gummi Worm is elastic? Why or why not?

You can calculate the percentage of growth that your Gummi Worm experienced by using this ratio: $\frac{\text{Stretched length} - \text{Original length}}{\text{Original length}} \times 100 = \%$ of growth. Show your work in the space provided.

Our work:

Our Gummi Worm had _____ % of growth.

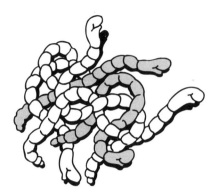

Gummi Worms: An Experiment in Variation

Class Data Sheet

Number of Students	Less than 10	10.1	10.2	10.3	10.4	10.5	10.6	10.7	10.8	10.9	11 or greater

Total Length (in centimeters)

Based on this class data,

The mean length of a Gummi Worm is _____

The median length of a Gummi Worm is _____

The mode is _____

WHAT HAPPENED 1,000,000 SECONDS AGO?

TEACHER'S PLANNING INFORMATION

Suggestions for Instruction

Ask students, "What happened 1 million seconds ago?" Write all of the answers down on the board or on an overhead transparency and discuss the wide variation in estimates. "Why is this question so difficult to answer? Can we understand the concept of 1 million seconds? Why?" The unit of seconds is inappropriate when the amount of time is so long! It is the same as asking someone, "How many inches is it from New York City to San Francisco?" It is difficult to visualize extremely large measurements using a very small unit of measure.

Allow students, working in pairs, time to solve the problem. Then find out what happened 1 *billion* seconds ago—this is 1,000 times longer than 1 million ($1,000,000 = 10^6$; $1,000,000,000 = 10^9$).

Students will probably be able to tell you what happened 1 million seconds ago but will have some difficulty with 1 billion seconds (about 32 years). It is difficult to find a particular year on the Internet, but a wonderful site to find references to what happened on a particular day is http://www.historychannel.com/tdih/tdih.jsp?category=leadstory

Another very interesting Web site is http://www.actionbioscience.org/education/lewis_lampe_lloyd.html. It help students understand the magnitude of geologic time by converting prehistoric time periods into equivalent distances on a football field (e.g., 3,800 million years ago ≈ 15 yards 20 inches or 12 years in an average human life span of 76 years).

> **Math Topics**
>
> Measurement of time, computation, problem solving
>
> **Active Learning**
>
> Students will
>
> 1. Compute length of time using appropriate units
>
> 2. Work collaboratively to problem solve a solution
>
> 3. Research historical connections
>
> **Materials**
>
> Calculators, What Happened 1,000,000 Seconds Ago? Worksheets, access to reference materials or Internet Web sites

Selected Answers

1,000,000 seconds is about 11 1/2 days.

1,000,000,000 seconds is about 32 years.

Variation

The next logical extension is to find out what happened 1 trillion seconds ago, or 10^{12} seconds. This was before written history, during prehistoric times. It is an interesting extension to have students explore.

Writing in Math

Journal questions:

1. Describe the methods you used to express 1 million seconds using more appropriate units of measure.

2. You are told that the distance between New York City and Chicago is approximately 45,000,000 inches. Just how many miles apart are these two cities?

What Happened 1,000,000 Seconds Ago?

Worksheet

Name _____

Date _____ Class _____

We don't usually use seconds to describe really long periods of time. But suppose we did? How long ago was 1,000,000 seconds (using a more appropriate unit of measure, such as days or months or years)? What were you doing 1,000,000 seconds ago? Work with your partner and a calculator to answer this question. Show your work and write your answer in the spaces provided.

Our work:

1,000,000 seconds ago was _____

What happened 1,000,000 seconds ago? _____

Now that you've figured that out, work with your partner to determine how long ago 1,000,000,000 (1 billion) seconds ago was. What was happening 1,000,000,000 seconds ago? What year was it? Were you born? This one may take a little more work. Show your work and write your answer in the spaces provided.

Our work:

1,000,000,000 seconds ago was _____

What happened 1,000,000,000 seconds ago? _____

HOW LONG WOULD IT TAKE TO WALK TO CHINA— THROUGH THE CENTER OF THE EARTH?

TEACHER'S PLANNING INFORMATION

Math Topics

Measurement, data collection and analysis, computation

Active Learning

Students will

1. Work collaboratively to problem solve a solution

2. Compute the diameter of the Earth

3. Problem solve the rate at which they walk

4. Compute how long it would take them (on average) to walk through the center of the Earth

5. Make connections between math and science

Materials

For each group of four students: calculators, metersticks or other measuring instruments; masking tape; How Long Would It Take to Walk to China? Worksheets; one stopwatch

Suggestions for Instruction

If a globe is available, hold it up as you ask, "If you could walk straight through the Earth, do you think you would end up in China?" Students should realize that there is a large body of water on the other side. The problem for this lesson is, "How long would it take to walk through the Earth to the other side?"

To solve this problem, students need to be familiar with the distance formula as it is used to find rate: $R = \frac{D}{T}$; where R = rate of speed, D = distance traveled, and T = time. Explain that a variation of the distance formula is used to determine how quickly a person walks. Rate is determined by dividing the distance one travels by the time it takes to get there. In other words, if you travel 10 miles (distance) in 2 hours (time), your rate is 5 mi/hr (rate).

Place students into groups of four with students rotating through the following roles:

(1) Recorder: This student records the data in the student worksheet data collection table.

(2) Timer: This student records the time it takes for students to walk a predetermined distance.

(3) Calculator: This students uses the calculator to make necessary computations.

(4) Organizer: This student measures the initial number of meters walked and marks it out using masking tape.

Before students proceed with the activity, explain that they need to walk a predetermined distance while timing the walk. Ask the group, "Do you think that the accuracy of the timing might be affected by the distance you choose? Why or why not?" Try to encourage students to choose a long enough distance so that the stopwatches can be used effectively. It is very difficult to time short amounts of time accurately because the shorter the distance, the greater the impact a person's reaction time makes.

Once each student's time has been established, the group has two of the three variables defined: distance and time. By applying the revised distance formula, each student's rate can be calculated.

A very unusual Web site, http://www.digholes.com/, allows you to enter your city, state, and zip code and see where you would end up if you walked through the center of the Earth. Could there be a more appropriate site?

Selected Answers

Answers will vary.

Variation

This activity combines two measurements—time and distance. Students can compute how long it would take them to walk (1) around the Earth—at the equator it's approximately 40,000 km—or (2) to the moon—approximately 406,700 km.

Writing in Math

Journal questions:

1. The distance between London and Paris is approximately 335,000 meters. If you could walk between these two famous cities, how long would it take using your group's average rate of speed?

2. The polar circumference (the distance around the Earth measured from the North Pole to the South Pole) is approximately 40,000 kilometers or 40,000,000 meters. How long would it take to walk around the Earth if you started at the North Pole and continued until you returned to the same place and walked at your group's average rate of speed?

How Long Would It Take to Walk to China—Through the Center of the Earth?

Worksheet

If you could walk straight through the Earth, do you think you would end up in China? Not if you lived in the United States, you wouldn't! You would be in the middle of the southern portion of the Indian Ocean—not too far (as the crow flies) from Australia. How long would it take for you to walk there? To calculate this, you need a little bit of information:

The Earth is made of layers, the surface of which is a thin crust about 40 kilometers (km) thick. Under this is a layer of liquid rock called the *mantle*, which is about 2,870 km thick. The mantle surrounds the outer core of the center of the Earth. Made of liquid iron and nickel, the outer core is about 2,100 km thick. In the center of the Earth is the inner core. Scientists believe the inner core is a solid ball of iron and nickel that is about 1,370 km to its center. This gets us to the center of the Earth!

How far is it from the surface to the center of the Earth? _____

How far is it from the surface to the center and back to the surface? _____

Now, let's get to the problem: How long would it take you to walk through the layers of the Earth to the center and then back out again to the surface?

Directions: Work with your group to find out how long it would take (as an average) to walk 1 kilometer. This will help you compute how long it will take you to get from your home to the Indian Ocean by walking the diameter of the Earth, right through the middle. Enter your data in the following table.

Name	Distance Walked (in meters)	Time	Rate $R = \frac{D}{T}$	Time to Walk Through the Earth

Show your work on the back of this page.

HEIGHT VERSUS SHOE LENGTH

TEACHER'S PLANNING INFORMATION

Suggestions for Instruction

Read with students the questions asked in the introduction on the students' pages: "Do you think there is a relationship between people's height and the size of their feet?" Explain that when the relationship between two variables is the same (for example, when one variable gets larger, the other gets larger), we say there is a positive or direct correlation. Ask students to give examples of other relationships that could be described as having a positive or direct correlation. For example, the circumference of a circle becomes greater as the diameter becomes greater or the amount of distance traveled increases with the amount of time one is traveling. This is an example of a graph of a direct variation. Notice that the shape of the graph clearly indicates the relationship between the two variables.

It is also a good idea to discuss indirect or negative correlation at this time. Indirect correlation is when one variable increases or becomes greater, the second becomes smaller. For example, as the temperature in a room rises, the volume of an ice cube in a glass becomes smaller, or the faster you drive, the less time it will take to get to your destination.

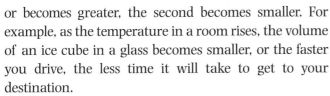

Direct Variation

Math Topics

Measurement, data collection and analysis, scatterplots, positive correlation (direct variation), ratios, mathematical constants, problem solving

Active Learning

Students will

1. Work collaboratively to take measurements to the nearest 1/10 centimeter

2. Calculate the ratio of height to foot length

3. Problem solve the horizontal and vertical units for a graph

4. Graph data on the coordinate plane

5. Analyze the scatterplot to ascertain if the class data shows a correlation between the two and, if so, if it is positive or negative (direct or indirect)

Materials

Metric tape measures or metersticks and metric rulers; one copy of Shoe Size Versus Height Data Collection Sheet for each group of four students; overhead transparency of Class Data Sheet; overhead transparency of graph

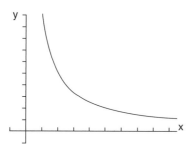

Here is an example of a graph of an indirect variation.

The graph that is produced using the student's data from this activity will resemble the example of direct variation.

After student groups have taken their measurements and recorded their data, each member of the group will enter his or her name on the Class Data Collection Sheet indicating the decimal ratio calculated from their measurements. The average or mean decimal ratio can be calculated and considered a *mathematical constant*. Ask students, "Can this number be used to estimate what a person's height might be if we know the foot size?"

Once all of the students' data is entered in the class table, problem solve with students what units would be appropriate on the horizontal and vertical axes of the graph. Find the range of data and divide by the number of units to calculate an appropriate size for each unit. Be sure to have students work on this problem, as this is a skill that is often overlooked since most graphs already supply these units.

When the graph is completed, ask students if the coordinates appear to be graphed in any particular direction: for example, from the upper right to the lower left or from the lower left to the upper right. Or perhaps the students see no pattern and the coordinates are randomly placed on the coordinate plane. As was discussed previously, while there will be some variation, in general, the data should show a positive correlation: as the height of the students increase, so do the size or length of their feet.

Selected Answers

Answers will vary.

Variation

Students, working in groups, can design an experiment in which they believe there would be a negative or indirect variation.

Writing in Math

Journal questions:

1. Discuss what is meant by a positive (direct) or negative (indirect) correlation. Give an example of each type of correlation. Be as precise as possible.

2. Give an example of two variables that when graphed would show no correlation at all. What would the scatterplot look like?

Height Versus Shoe Length

Worksheet

Name _____

Date _____ Class _____

Do you think there is a relationship between how tall people are and their hand spans or the length of their shoes? Why? Today we are going to conduct a measurement experiment to see if your predictions are accurate. Be sure to follow each of these directions carefully and be as accurate as you can with your measurement.

Directions:

1. Using metersticks or the metric tape measure, very carefully measure the height of each person in your group. Round your measurement to the nearest centimeter (cm).

2. First remove your shoes, then measure the foot length of each person to the nearest 1/10 cm.

3. Find the decimal ratio: $\frac{\text{Height}}{\text{Foot Length}}$. Round this number to the nearest 1/10.

4. When everyone in the group has completed the measurements and calculations, enter your data on the Class Data transparency.

Name	Height (nearest centimeter)	Foot Length (nearest 1/10 centimeter)	Ratio $\frac{\text{Height}}{\text{Foot Length}}$	Decimal Ratio (Round to 1/10)
MEAN				

Height Versus Shoe Length

Scatterplot Graph of the Data

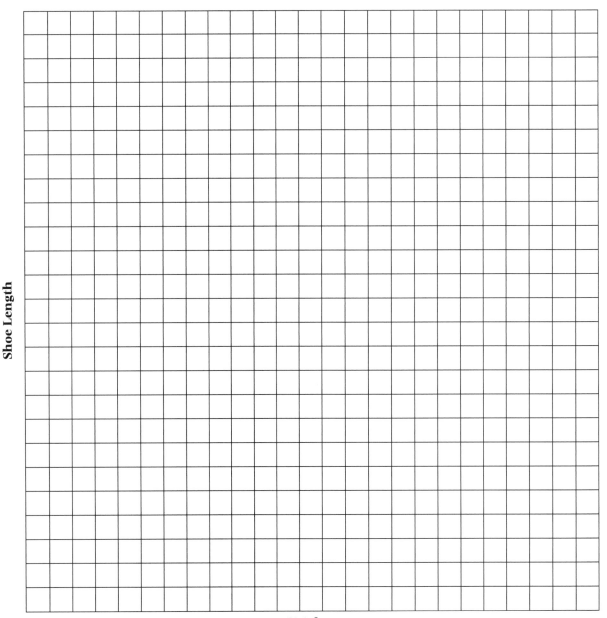

Shoe Length

Height

EGGSCETERA

TEACHER'S PLANNING INFORMATION

Suggestions for Instruction

Students work in groups of four to find the circumference, mass, and height of each of their eggs. The collected data is used to answer the questions on Worksheet 2. To find the percentage of increase (difference), the following formula is used: $\frac{\text{difference}}{\text{original measurement}} \times 100$. Use the measurement of the smaller of the two eggs to find the percentage of increase.

Hard boil enough eggs of each size so that each group will have one of each size. Supply student groups with the worksheets. Prepare an overhead transparency of the Class Data Table to find the average circumference, mass, and height of each of the sizes. These averages are used to compare the relationship that may or may not exist between the size of the egg and the price. For example, if medium eggs are selling for 69¢ a dozen, or 5.75¢ each, and large eggs are selling for 89¢ a dozen, or 7.4¢ each, the difference is 1.65¢. The ratio of increase to the cost of the medium eggs is 1.65¢/69¢, or .02 (.02 × 100 equals 2%). If the percentage of difference in the size of the eggs is less than 2%, then buying the smaller egg is a better buy; if the percentage of difference between the sizes is greater than 2%, then the larger egg is the better buy. By using average sizes, these computations can be performed by the entire class.

The federal government has very strict guidelines regarding the weight of eggs as it relates to their size. The following table reflects the data collected from the USDA Web site. It was given in ounces and was

Math Topics

Measurement (linear and mass), decimals, whole number operations, percentage of difference, consumer pricing (best buy), estimation, circumference, formulas

Active Learning

Students will

1. Measure circumference of objects to the nearest millimeter and compare them

2. Determine the mass of objects and compare them

3. Problem solve to find the height of the eggs to the nearest millimeter

4. Find the difference of the measurements

5. Find the percentage of difference of the measurements

6. Determine the relationship between the size of a product and its cost

Materials

For each group of students: EggsCetera Worksheets 1 and 2; one each medium, large, and jumbo hard-boiled egg; one scale; one tape measure with metric measurements; and rulers; also, calculators, overhead transparency of the Class Data Table

Jumbo	30 oz/doz	2.5 oz/each	≈ 70 g
Large	24 oz/doz	2 oz	≈ 55 g
Medium	21 oz/doz	1.75 oz	≈ 50 g

SOURCE: http://www.ams.usda.gov/poultry/standards/AMS-EggSt-1995.htm#UnitedStatesConsumer GradesandWeight

converted to grams, to be consistent in the use of metric measurements. The metric weights have been rounded to the nearest 5 grams.

On http://www.aeb.org/KidsAndFamily/billions_and_billions_of_broken_ .htm, there is an interesting problem to share with your students. It is about a machine that breaks 108,000 eggs per hour, and students are asked to calculate how many eggs are broken each second. However, the site gives the answer and a way to solve it, so you might want to read it first and then share it with them.

Selected Answers

Answers will vary.

Variation

Have students find the better buy by researching small, medium, and large sizes of other products, such as detergents, cereals, and milk.

Writing in Math

Journal questions:

1. If large eggs are selling for 79¢ a dozen and jumbo eggs are selling for $1.29 a dozen, how much more are you paying for each jumbo egg than each large egg? What percent of difference is this? Explain how you solved this problem.

2. Jumbo eggs weigh approximately 30 oz/doz and large eggs weigh approximately 24 oz/doz. The supermarket is selling jumbo eggs for $2.59/doz and large eggs for $1.69/doz. Which is the better buy and why?

EggsCetera

Worksheet I

Name _____

Date _____ Class _____

Have you ever wondered why there are so many different sizes of eggs? Is one size a better buy than the others? Are jumbo eggs so much bigger than medium eggs that they are worth the increased price? What do you think? _____

How much bigger are they? _____

How much more do you think they weigh? _____

The experiment we will be conducting today will help us understand the differences in the sizes of eggs.

Directions: Working in groups of four, take three different measurements: (1) Circumference— The circumference is the distance around the egg at the widest point; (2) Mass (be sure to record the mass in the correct place in the table); and (3) Height. Record each measurement in the space provided on your data collection table.

Cooperate to get the most accurate measurements possible!

Size of Egg	*Circumference* (in centimeters)	*Mass* (in grams)	*Height* (in centimeters)
Medium			
Large			
Jumbo			

EggsCetera

Worksheet 2

Name _____

Date _____ Class _____

Use the data you have collected to answer these questions:

Question	Difference	Percentage of Difference $\dfrac{\text{Diffierence}}{\text{Measurement of Smaller Egg}} \times 100$
What is the difference between the circumference of the medium and the large egg?		
What is the difference between the circumference of the medium and the jumbo egg?		
What is the difference between the circumference of the large and the jumbo egg?		
What is the difference between the mass of the medium and the large egg?		
What is the difference between the mass of the medium and the jumbo egg?		
What is the difference between the mass of the large and the jumbo egg?		
What is the difference between the height of the medium and the large egg?		
What is the difference between the height of the medium and the jumbo egg?		
What is the difference between the height of the large and the jumbo egg?		

EggsCetera

Class Data Table

Group	Circumference			Mass			Height		
	Medium	Large	Jumbo	Medium	Large	Jumbo	Medium	Large	Jumbo
1									
2									
3									
4									
5									
6									
7									
8									
9									
10									
Class Mean									

Something to think about . . .

1 dozen medium eggs cost 79¢

1 dozen large eggs cost 98¢

1 dozen jumbo eggs cost $1.09

What's the best buy? Why? _____

_____

Data Collection and Probability 5

Data Collection and Probability 5

Misunderstanding of probability may be the greatest of all impediments to scientific literacy.

—Stephen Jay Gould

We live in an age of technology where the information explosion requires us to not only understand how data is collected but also how it is processed, translated into usable knowledge, and used to make predictions and decisions. John Allen Paulos (2001) maintained that the combination of our inability to deal with massive quantities of data and our misconceptions about the laws of probability have resulted in misinformed government policies and poorly planned personal decisions.

Statistical activities should develop students' appreciation of how data is used in the real world. The process should take students through four processes:

- Collection
- Organization
- Analysis
- Graphic representation

Students should collect data to elicit relevant personal information. The investigation should help students better understand their world and themselves. Students should look for patterns or trends, and "what if" questions must be asked. Graphing allows students to present the data that has been sorted and classified and is a natural extension of the organization phase. The National Council of Teachers of Mathematics (2000) recommends that students formulate questions that can be addressed with data; collect, organize, and display relevant data to answer their questions; use appropriate statistics to analyze data; and use data to make predictions. In addition, students should be able to understand and apply the basic concepts of probability, develop an understanding of chance, and be able to determine the likelihood of an event.

The investigations in this chapter take students through all the steps of the data collection process, relate inquiries to real-world applications, and use simulations as a means to get students actively involved in mathematics.

SUPER SURVEY

Super Survey is an open-ended problem that allows students to move through a complete data collection activity. The students design a question that is of interest to them and then organize the responses in a frequency table. By computing the ratio and percentages, students begin the process of analyzing their data. Last, a graph is constructed and examined.

WHAT IS YOUR FAVORITE SUBJECT?

Some surveys require greater organization of the data for future analysis; What Is Your Favorite Subject? is an example of such a survey. Students do not give the participants choices but rather allow for free response. These responses need to be categorized, grouped, and analyzed. Allowing students to make two different types of graphs encourages them to evaluate both in order to determine which better represents the data collected. Is one graph a better choice than the other?—a good question to respond to in a journal question, perhaps.

STARS OF THE NBA

This activity uses statistical information to help students understand the importance of graphic representation in the analysis of data. Box-and-whisker plots are used to understand and analyze the average points per game and field goal percentages of the top NBA players, and a scatterplot is used to uncover the relationship between two other statistical variables, total points and total rebounds.

DICE AND PROBABILITY

Dice and Probability involves a difficult concept—why is there a greater chance of one sum appearing than any other? Students are required to compute the probability of an event by calculating all the possible outcomes of tossing a pair of dice. Because $2 + 5$, $5 + 2$, $4 + 3$, $3 + 4$, $1 + 6$, and $6 + 1$ have the same sum, they account for six different outcomes. By working together and discussing their findings, students increase their understanding of the mathematical concept of chance.

IS THIS GAME FAIR?

What is a fair game? Is This Game Fair? investigates that question. After students predict if the game is fair, they gather necessary information to analyze and modify their original predictions on the basis of this new data. This type of activity is fundamental to developing higher-level reasoning. Interesting discussions can be conducted in the mathematics classroom!

DINOSAURS AND PROBABILITY

Dinosaurs and Probability is an activity that encourages students to use collected data to make predictions and helps them understand the power of mathematics. With this activity, the correctness of the students' answers is not immediately evident. Students need to gather additional information to determine the validity of their original predictions.

SUPER SURVEY

TEACHER'S PLANNING INFORMATION

Math Topics

Data collection, organization, analysis, circle graphs, ratio, percentage, measurement

Active Learning

Students will

1. Design a survey question, including choices for responses

2. Question 36 fellow students to collect data

3. Organize data in a frequency table

4. Compute frequency, ratio, percentage, and degrees needed to produce a circle graph

5. Create a circle graph of the data

Materials

Super Survey Worksheets for each student; protractors; calculators; markers, crayons, or colored pencils; rulers

Suggestions for Instruction

Ask students, "Why do we take surveys? What characteristics of the questions and choices make a survey more accurate? Why must we think carefully about the choices we give the respondents?" It is important that students understand that the way they phrase the questions and choices can make the results more accurate. Give them this example: "Suppose a person wants to survey people's favorite automobiles. Their question is, "From these five choices, what would you pick as your favorite automobile?" The choices given are Chevrolet, Buick, Ford, Mercury, and Porsche. Ask, "What's wrong with this survey? Do you think that the choices might influence the results? What other problems do you see? Do you have any other examples of questions or choices that might unfairly affect the results of a survey?" Take time to discuss these problems with students and explain that very often, surveys are designed to influence the results and the "buyer must beware!"

Students will need a day to circulate the survey and enter their results in the table. The next day in class, give them protractors, rulers, and markers to design their graphs. Give them freedom to develop their own procedures to convert the percentage of number of people to the necessary number of degrees in the angles of the circle graph. There are a number of ways they can solve this, and they should be given the opportunity to use the method that makes the most sense to them.

An interesting Web site introduces students to the census and counting populations. It is http://www.education-world.com/a_lesson/lesson173.shtml

The National Center for Educational Statistics has an interesting site that has suggestions about making graphs, taking surveys, and probability. It is http://nces.ed.gov/nceskids/Games.asp

Selected Answers

Answers will vary.

Variation

If you wish to simplify the activity, have students interview only 20 people. Cutting the number of responses makes it easier to find the percentages and not too much more difficult to compute the number of degrees needed to draw the angles in the circle graph.

Writing in Math

Journal questions:

1. I am doing a survey and my question is, "What is your favorite snake?" I am giving the respondent the following choices: garden snake, python, rattlesnake, and spitting cobra. Do you think the quality of my choices is good or bad? Why?

2. Design a survey question and choices in a way that might influence the outcome of the survey. Explain your reasoning.

Super Survey

Worksheet 1: Data Collection

Name _____

Date _____ Class _____

You are going to conduct a survey. Choose a question carefully and write it out in full in the space provided. It is important that you ask the question of each person in the same way, so do write it out. Choose four to six choices that you will give the respondents. List the choices. Interview exactly 36 people.

My question: _____

My choices:

1. _____

2. _____

3. _____

4. _____

5. _____

6. _____

Choices	Tally	Frequency	Fraction $\frac{n}{36}$	Percent	Degrees of Circle $\frac{n}{360°}$

Super Survey

Worksheet 2: Graph

Name _____

Date _____ Class _____

Describe some interesting facts about your data that are shown in this graph:

_____

_____

_____

_____

WHAT IS YOUR FAVORITE SUBJECT?

TEACHER'S PLANNING INFORMATION

Suggestions for Instruction

The previous activity, Super Survey, allowed the students to supply their survey respondents with four or five choices, thereby making the organization a simpler process. In this activity, students can choose any subject they want and so the interviewer must first organize the responses into categories before tallying the results. Also discuss with students that although they are not giving respondents particular choices, they must still be careful that they interview a wide variety of students to get a representative sample of the school.

Students can work alone or in groups of two. Have them survey at least 20 students. The survey question is, "What is your favorite subject?" The responses and the gender of the respondents are recorded in the table provided. Make sure students understand that the data has to be organized before it is recorded in the frequency table. If the students wish to combine some subjects for ease of reporting, they must justify their decisions in their paragraphs. The results are reported by ratio and percentage of girls and boys. Some attempt should be made to describe preference as a gender issue. The final step is graphing the results on a circle graph as well as a bar graph. The units for each graph are to be designed by the students. If students work in pairs, you might request a separate graph from each student, thereby giving each student practice in determining units and making graphs.

Math Topics

Data collection, organization, analysis, bar and circle graphs, measurement, percentage

Active Learning

Students will

1. Collect nonstructured data

2. Organize the data into a frequency table

3. Graph the data using two different graphs

Materials

What Is Your Favorite Subject? Worksheets 1–4, protractors and rulers, colored pencils or markers

Selected Answers

Answers will vary.

Variation

Students can increase the number of variables by asking boys and girls in two or more grades. This makes the organization of the data more complicated, but it permits students to make comparisons between children of different ages.

Writing in Math

Journal questions:

1. Describe the results of your survey and analyze any differences in the preferences of students (boys vs. girls, grade level differences, etc.).

2. Suppose you wanted to randomly choose students in your school to survey. Do you think it would be a good idea to interview students in your lunchroom? Why or why not?

What Is Your Favorite Subject Set?

Worksheet 1: Data Collection

Name _____

Date _____ Class _____

Name	Gender (male or female)	Subject

What Is Your Favorite Subject?

Worksheet 2: Frequency Table of Results

Subject	Number of Boys	Number of Girls	Ratio of Boys	Ratio of Girls	Percentage of Boys	Percentage of Girls

What subject appeared to be the most popular with boys? _____

What subject appeared to be the most popular with girls? _____

Use a separate piece of paper to write an article for the school newspaper about your survey. The article should be a couple of paragraphs long and should be composed with well-written sentences that accurately describe the results of your survey. *Who* did you survey; *what* did they tell you; *why* is this of interest to the school; and *how* did you choose the students who answered your questions?

What Is Your Favorite Subject?

Worksheet 3: Bar Graph of Data

Name _____

Date _____ Class _____

NUMBER OF STUDENTS

20
19
18
17
16
15
14
13
12
11
10
9
8
7
6
5
4
3
2
1

SUBJECTS

What Is Your Favorite Subject?

Worksheet 4: Circle Graphs of Data

Name _____

Date _____ Class _____

BOYS

Which of the graphs (the bar or circle graphs) do you think is a better representation of the data you collected? Explain your answer. _____

_____

_____

_____

_____

_____

_____

GIRLS

Did you find a definite subject preference between the boys and the girls you surveyed? If yes, how might you explain the differences? _____

_____

_____

_____

_____

_____

_____

STARS OF THE NBA

TEACHER'S PLANNING INFORMATION

Suggestions for Instruction

Give each pair of students a copy of the statistics in Table 5.5. Some students may not be familiar with basketball, and some discussion may be needed to explain the meaning of the statistics. Explain that the data list an average or mean for each player. Additional information is available on individual teams and players on the official NBA Web site: http://www.nba.com/statistics.

Although Stars of the NBA Worksheet 1 requires student's names, a scatterplot of the points per game data is made for them, step by step. Go through each step so that students understand the process of making a box-and-whisker plot. Some review of the term *median* may be necessary.

Point out to students that when the points were listed from least to greatest in the first step, there was the same number of data in each quadrant. And yet when the box-and-whisker plot was drawn, the quadrants were not all the same size. The first quadrant (between 21 and 22) contains four pieces of data, as does the fourth quadrant (between 27.6 and 34). Ask students, "Why does the graph look like it does? Why are all of the quadrants not the same size?" Discuss with students the uniqueness of this graphic representation: The size of each quadrant is dependent on the *range* of the data, not the number of pieces of data.

When students understand the procedure for making the graph, give each pair of students a copy of Worksheets 2 and 3. The data needed to answer the questions and draw the graph is in Table 5.6 on Worksheet 3. The answers to the questions on Worksheet 2 can be found under Selected Answers.

Math Topics

Data collection and analysis, graphic representation, statistics

Active Learning

Students will

1. Work collaboratively to analyze data

2. Find means, medians, and modes

3. Draw a box-and-whisker plot of the data

4. Draw a scatterplot of data

5. Examine the graphs and draw conclusions based upon the shape of the graphs

Materials

Copies of Stars of the NBA Worksheets 1–4 for each pair of students, overhead transparency of Worksheets 1 and 4, overhead transparency of Stars of the NBA: Points per Game and Field Goal Percentage data table (and copies of this sheet for each pair of students), calculators, rulers

Students may have difficulty finding the units to use on the scatterplot graph; a good strategy is to count the number of spaces, find the range of the data, and calculate reasonable units for both the horizontal and vertical axes. While it is recommended that each group problem solve appropriate units, if a group is having difficulty, these units will work: for the horizontal axis (total rebounds), units of 10 will work; on the vertical axis (total points), units of 20 will work.

A site that is hosted by Utah State University, the National Library of Virtual Manipulatives, has a wide variety of graphic representation and probability experiments. It is: http://www.shodor.org/interactivate/activities/prob/index.html.

Selected Answers

Worksheet 2:

1. .333, .406, .463, .464, .476, .480, .496, .497, .516, .524, .524, .545, .551, .560, .573, .609

2. The range

3. The median of the data is 506.5.

4. The lower quartile is .470.

5. The upper quartile is .548.

6. Of the data, 50% is in the box; 25% is in the lower quartile and 25% is in the upper quartile.

7. The size of each quartile is determined by the range of the data, not the number of pieces of data—the smaller the quartile, the smaller the range of data.

Scatterplot:

The scatterplot shown here has units of 10 on the horizontal axis and of 20 on the vertical axis. Students may choose different units, but the shape of the graphs should be similar. It will not be identical because points are placed on approximate coordinates. Also, a line that seems to reflect the trend of the data has been drawn. It appears that there is a weak positive correlation between total points scored and total rebounds.

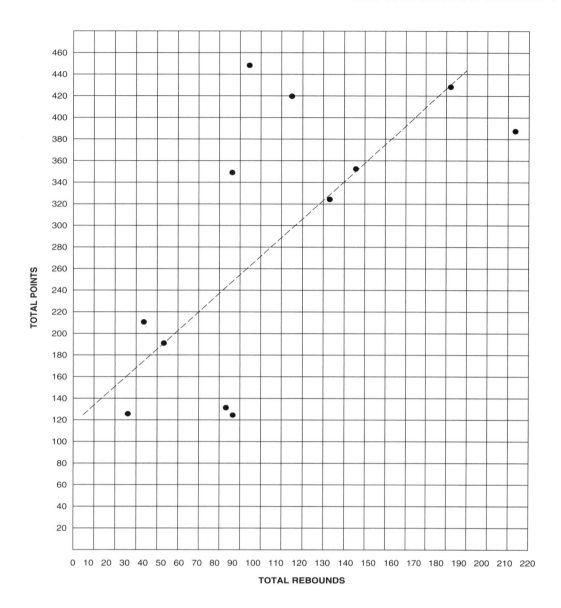

Variation

Two interesting sports statistics to compare are batting averages and slugging percentages—batting averages are based on the ratio of the number of hits to total at bats, but slugging percentages weight the type of hits (the more bases attained on a hit, the more points earned). These are the two formulas: $\text{Batting average} = \frac{\text{number of hits}}{\text{at bats}}$. Slugging percentage is found using the following formula: $\text{Slugging percentage} = \frac{s + 2d + 3t + 4h}{\text{at bats}}$, where s = singles, d = doubles, t = triples, and h = home runs. Students can get the statistics from the major league baseball Web site, http://mlb.mlb.com/ NASApp/mlb/index.jsp, and use it to make box-and-whisker plots on the same page and compare the two graphs.

Writing in Math

Journal questions:

1. Explain in your own words how you organized the data to design a box-and-whisker plot.

2. Use the data in the table to design a box-and-whisker plot. Explain what steps you took to draw the graph.

City	Mean High Temperature in July ($^{\circ}$F)
San Francisco, CA	71°
Birmingham, AL	88°
Fairbanks, AK	72°
Phoenix, AZ	105°
Key West, FL	88°
Honolulu, HI	87°
Chicago, IL	84°
New Orleans, LA	90°
Boston, MA	81°
Albuquerque, NM	90°

SOURCE: Information obtained from http://www.countrystudies.us/united-states/weather/

Stars of the NBA:
Points per Game and
Field Goal Percentages

Worksheet

The leading 14 scorers of the NBA during the 2005–2006 season are listed in the following table.. Also listed are their field goal percentages. One of the statistics tell us the average number of points that were scored per game, and the other speaks to the efficiency of scoring—the ratio of field goal attempts to field goal made. We are going to make two interesting graphs of this data to help with our analysis.

Player's Name	Team Name	Average Points per Game	Field Goal Percentage
Gilbert Arenas	Washington	34.0	.464
LeBron James	Cleveland	30.8	.476
Vince Carter	New Jersey Nets	29.6	.463
Kobe Bryant	Los Angeles Lakers	27.9	.497
Dirk Nowitzki	Dallas	27.3	.496
Michael Redd	Milwaukee	27.2	.524
Dwayane Wade	Miami	27.0	.516
Tim Duncan	San Antonio Spurs	25.8	.573
Elton Brand	Los Angeles Clippers	25.4	.551
Bonzi Wells	Sacramento	23.2	.609
Andres Nocioni	Chicago	22.3	.560
Richard Jefferson	New Jersey Nets	22.2	.545
Tony Parker	San Antonio Spurs	21.1	.480
Carmelo Anthony	Denver	21.0	.333
Ben Gordon	Chicago	21.0	.406
Jermaine O'Neal	Indiana	21.0	.524

SOURCE: Data obtained from http://www.nba.com/statistics/player/Scoring.jsp. Reprinted with permission of NBA Entertainment.

Do any of these players stand out as more accurate? Why or why not? What statistic did you use to help you with this problem?

Stars of the NBA: Points per Game and Field Goal Percentages

Worksheet 1: The Box-and-Whisker Plots

Name _____

Date _____ Class _____

The box-and-whisker plot representing the points per game is shown in the figure that follows. The directions for each step are given. After you understand the procedures used to draw this interesting graph, use the data for field goal percentage to draw another box-and-whisker plot. Use the two graphs to help you answer the questions.

To design a box-and-whisker plot, these are the steps:

1. Rewrite the average points scored: 21.0, 21.0, 21.0, 21.1, 22.2, 22.3, 23.2, 25.4, 25.8, 27.0, 27.2, 27.3, 27.9, 29.6, 30.8, 34.0

2. The "whisker" of the box-and-whisker plot represents the lowest and highest scores. A line connects the two scores—*the whisker.*

3. The *median* score of the data is found. Since there are 16 scores, the median is the average of the 8th and the 9th scores or 25.6. A line is drawn above that coordinate on the whisker.

4. Find the *lower quartile* or the median of the lower half of the data; this score is between the 4th and 5th scores or 21.15. A line is drawn above that coordinate.

5. Find the *upper quartile* or the median of the upper half of the data; this score is between the 27.3 and the 27.9 or 27.6. A line is drawn above that coordinate.

6. Draw a line to connect the tops and bottoms of the lines that designate the upper quartile, the lower quartile, and the median. You have now formed the *box* of the box-and-whisker plot.

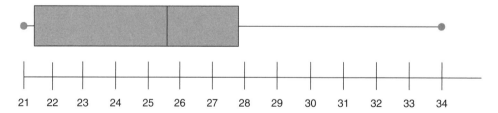

Follows these steps and use the data supplied for the field goal percentages to design a box-and-whisker plot on the following page.

Stars of the NBA:
Points per Game and
Field Goal Percentages

Worksheet 2:
The Box-and-Whisker Plots

Name _____

Date _____ Class _____

Use the list of NBA statistics to help you answer these questions and complete the graph.

1. List field goal percentages from least to greatest: _____

2. What statistic do these two coordinates represent? _____ Use this range to compute the units that you will use on the graph (they must all be equal). Write these units on the graph that follows. (HINT: The first two have been done for you.)

    Draw dots for the highest and lowest percentages above the correct coordinates on the number line. Draw the "whisker" to connect these two points.

3. Find the median of the data. (Since there are 16 statistics, you will need to find the average.) The median of the data is: _____ Draw a line on the whisker above that coordinate.

4. Find the lower quartile. (Again you will need to find the average.) The lower quartile is: _____. Draw a line on the whisker above that coordinate.

5. Find the upper quartile. (Again you will need to find the average.) The upper quartile is: _____. Draw a line on the whisker above that coordinate.

6. Draw a line to connect the tops and bottoms of the lines that designate the upper quartile, the lower quartile, and the median. You have now formed the box of the box-and-whisker plot.

What percentage of the data is in the box? _____

In the upper quartile? _____

In the lower quartile? _____

If each section of the box-and-whisker plot represents the same number of data, why are they not all the same size? _____

325 350

Stars of the NBA: Total Points and Rebounds

Worksheet 3

Name _____

Date _____ Class _____

This table shows the total number of points and total rebounds of 12 NBA stars during the 2005/2006 season. Design a scatterplot on the grid on the next page to represent the data.

Player's Name	Team Name	Total Points	Total Rebounds
Gilbert Arenas	Washington	204	33
LeBron James	Cleveland	400	105
Dirk Nowitzki	Dallas	409	181
Vince Carter	New Jersey Nets	326	77
Tim Duncan	San Antonio Spurs	336	137
Elton Brand	Los Angeles Clippers	305	123
Kobe Bryant	Los Angeles Lakers	195	44
Dwayane Wade	Miami	432	84
Bonzi Wells	Sacramento	139	72
Lamar Odom	Los Angeles Lakers	134	77
Shawn Marion	Phoenix	374	212
Michael Redd	Milwaukee	136	27

SOURCE: Data obtained from http://www.nba.com/statistics/player/PRA.jsp. Reprinted with the permission of NBA Entertainment.

1. After you have completed drawing the scatterplot, describe the shape of the graph.

   _____

   _____

2. Does it appear that the relationship between point scored and rebounds is positive or negative? Explain your answer.

   _____

   _____

3. Do the statistics confirm what you know about the game of basketball? Why?

   _____

   _____

Stars of the NBA: Total Points and Rebounds

Scatterplot Graph

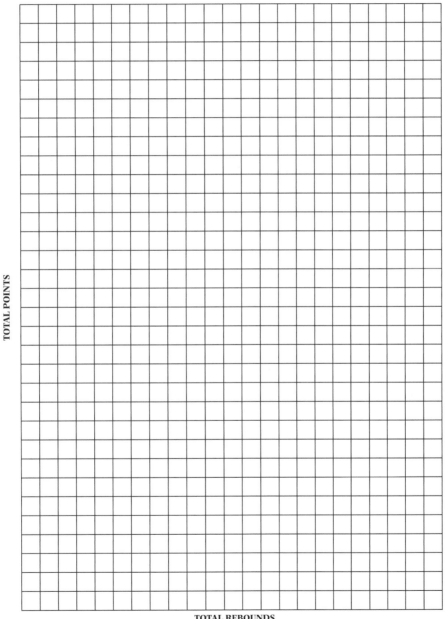

TOTAL POINTS

TOTAL REBOUNDS

DICE AND PROBABILITY

TEACHER'S PLANNING INFORMATION

Math Topics

Probability, data collection and analysis, fractions, percentages, graphing

Active Learning

Students will

1. Predict the outcome of a mathematical experiment

2. Work with a partner to conduct the experiment and analyze the results

3. Collect class results to further analyze the data

4. Draw a bar graph of their results

Materials

One pair of dice for each pair of students; One set of Pair of Dice and Probability Worksheets 1, 2, and 4 for each pair of students; overhead transparency of Worksheet 3

Suggestions for Instruction

Begin the discussion by asking students the following:

- What possible sums can appear when we roll a pair of dice?
- Do you think that each of the sums will appear the same number of times?
- What do you think will happen if we roll the dice 100 times?

If you wish, you can record the discussion on the blackboard or on newsprint. Students, working with a partner, continue working through the experiment. Your role is to act as a facilitator while the students collect their data. When the data collection is complete, record the group data on Worksheet 3 and work with students to find the means. The probability of each sum occurring relates to the number of possibilities each sum has to appear. A 6×6 matrix is a good way to show students all of the possible outcomes.

+	1	2	3	4	5	6
1	2	3	4	5	6	7
2	3	4	5	6	7	8
3	4	5	6	7	8	9
4	5	6	7	8	9	10
5	6	7	8	9	10	11
6	7	8	9	10	11	12

There is only one way to get a sum of 2; therefore, the probability of getting a sum of 2 is 1 out of 36, or 1/36; a sum of 3 is 2/36; and so on. Students can use ratio/proportion to figure out the theoretical probability of an event occurring. For example, the probability of a sum of 7 occurring is 6/36 or 1/6; so if the dice are tossed 100 times, the ratio would be $1/6 = x/100$, or about 17 occurrences. The bar graph will resemble the following graph.

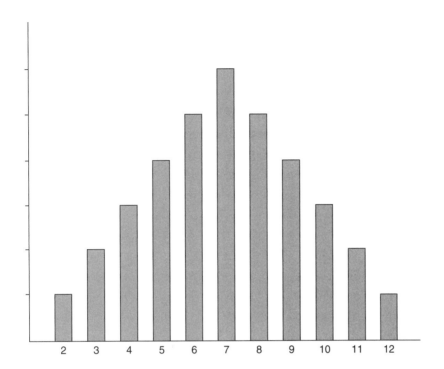

Have pairs of students divide up the tasks: one student rolls the dice while the other records the data. When they have collected their data, it is placed on Worksheet 3 for further analysis. The final task for each pair is to answer the questions that are part of the lesson and draw a bar graph of their results.

There are many games on the www.shodor.org/interactivate Web site, but one in particular gives students the opportunity to roll dice or spin spinners singly or in groups of 5 or 10 at a time. The program keeps track of the results as a tally. Other probability simulations on this site include horse races, the Monty Hall Game, and adjustable spinners.

Selected Answers

Answers will vary.

Variation

Students can conduct an experiment to determine how many tosses of the dice it takes before they get a sum of 7. Each group should conduct the experiment at least 10 times and find the average throws they needed to obtain this sum. Since the probability of getting a sum of 7 is 1/6, the odds of getting a sum of 7 is 1:5: One time out of 6 throws they will get a sum of 7 and 5 out of 6 tosses they will not. This is a good experiment to get students actively involved in learning the concept of odds and how odds relate to probability. The difference between odds and probability is reflected in these two formulas: $\text{Probability(x)} = \frac{\text{Chances for}}{\text{Total chances}}$; odds are calculated by (chances for) : (chances against).

Writing in Math

Journal questions:

1. Explain why there is not an equally likely probability that each sum will appear, based on the results of your experiment.

2. Design an experiment where there is an equally likely chance for each occurrence—making it a *fair game.*

Dice and Probability

Worksheet 1

Name _____

Date _____ Class _____

You and your partner will conduct an experiment. You will roll a pair of dice 100 times, find the sum, and record the results. Before rolling the dice, predict what you think will occur by answering these questions. Write down your predictions on the back of this page.

1. What are the possible things that can happen?

2. What do you predict will happen? Do you think one sum will appear more often than another? Why?

Now conduct the experiment. Record your results in the following table.

Sum of the dice	Tally	Frequency	Fraction	Percentage
2				
3				
4				
5				
6				
7				
8				
9				
10				
11				
12				
Total				

Dice and Probability

Worksheet 2

Name _____

Date _____ Class _____

Directions: Draw a graph of the data you collected during your experiment. Be sure to label the units on the vertical axis.

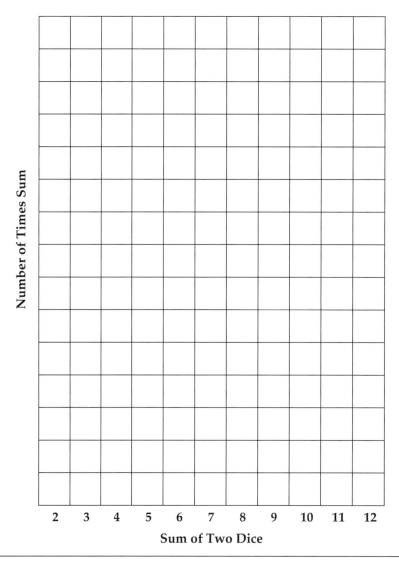

Number of Times Sum (vertical axis)

2 3 4 5 6 7 8 9 10 11 12

Sum of Two Dice

Dice and Probability

Worksheet 3: Class Data

Name _____

Date _____ Class _____

Record the number of times each of these sums appeared in your data.

Team	Sum of										
	2	3	4	5	6	7	8	9	10	11	12
A											
B											
C											
D											
E											
F											
G											
H											
I											
J											
K											
L											
M											
N											
O											
Means											

Dice and Probability

Worksheet 4

Name _____

Date _____ Class _____

Work with your partner to analyze the Dice and Probability experiment by answering these questions:

1. Does it appear that one sum occurs more often than others? Explain your answer.

_____

_____

_____

_____

2. Why do you think you got the results you did? Consider the different ways each of the sums can appear; for example, how many different ways can you obtain a sum of 2? A sum of 9? Which sum has the greatest chance because it has the largest number of combinations?

_____

_____

_____

_____

3. Think about what possible options or events there are when you roll only one die. Explain the difference in probability and chance when you roll a pair of dice and take the sum instead of just recording what number appears when you roll one die.

_____

_____

_____

IS THIS GAME FAIR?

TEACHER'S PLANNING INFORMATION

Suggestions for Instruction

Begin discussion by passing out game sheets (Worksheet 1, both pages) and reading the directions with the students. Allow students time to discuss whether or not they believe the game is fair. Bring the discussion around to the idea of fairness and what makes a game fair. Is it fair if you win? Does fair mean there is an equal chance of either player winning?

Once students have made their predictions, allow them time to play the game. The Worksheet allows for eight games to be played; each member of the group has a chance to be the player four times and the banker four times. The second page of the game sheet is provided to give students the opportunity to play all of the games. Instruct students to play as many games as they can within the allotted time. After each game, ask students to record whether the "player" or the "banker" won the game and to record the winner in the space provided.

When all groups are finished, record their results on the Class Record table for ease of analysis. The more games that are played, the better the chance that the experimental results will approach theoretical odds. Since the probability of obtaining a sum of 7 is $1/6$ ($6/36$), the odds are that five times the player will roll other than a sum of 7, and one time the faces will add up to a sum of 7. Ask the students to devise a game that is fair. One of the ways the game can be made fair is by having the banker pay the player $5 for each sum of 7 rolled.

Students begin by making their predictions and then, working in pairs, playing the maximum number of games they can in the time provided. After playing the game, pairs of students should analyze their predictions and make corrections, if necessary, based on their results. Each pair must determine how they would change the rules to make this game fair.

Math Topics

Probability, odds, data collection and analysis, problem solving

Active Learning

Students will

1. Work with a partner to simulate a game of chance

2. Analyze the concept of *fairness*

3. Predict whether or not a game is fair based on the payoff

4. Collect the necessary data to analyze their predictions and make corrections if necessary

5. Analyze the odds to determine how to make the game fair

Materials

One pair of dice for each pair of students, copies of Is This Game Fair? Worksheets 1 and 2, overhead transparency of Class Data Table

Selected Answers

Answers will vary.

Variation

This activity is designed for students who have had some experience with probability and odds. It is best to give fifth and sixth graders experiences rolling one die, spinning dials, or tossing coins.

Writing in Math

Journal question:

1. We are going to change the rules of the game as follows: The player wins if the sum on the dice is a multiple of three. What payoff would make this new game fair?

Is This Game Fair?

Worksheet 1, Page 1

Name _____

Date _____ Class _____

Directions: For this game there will be a "player" and a "banker." Each will start out with $10.00. The object of the game is to see who can win the most amount of money. Use the tables that follow to play the game using these rules:

1. Only the player rolls the dice. (Each successive game, you will take turns taking the role of player.)

2. The dice are tossed and the sum of the two faces is taken.

3. If the player rolls a sum of 7, the banker must pay the player $3.00.

4. If the player rolls other than a sum of 7, the player pays the banker only $1.00.

5. Circle if the player rolled a sum of 7; then add the correct amount of money to either the player's money or the banker's money *each time* the dice are rolled.

   Do you think this game is fair? Why or why not?

   Now play the game with your partner. Take turns being the "player" and the "banker." Play as many games as you can during the time allotted. It is possible to play eight games. When you have finished, reevaluate your original prediction as to the fairness of this game, and share your results with the class.

Is This Game Fair?

Worksheet 1, Page 2

	Starts with	Did the player roll a sum of 7? CIRCLE ONE										Who won?
		Yes or No	Yes or No	Yes or No	Yes or No	Yes or No	Yes or No	Yes or No	Yes or No	Yes or No	Yes or No	
Player	$10											
Banker	$10											

	Starts with	Did the player roll a sum of 7? CIRCLE ONE										Who won?
		Yes or No	Yes or No	Yes or No	Yes or No	Yes or No	Yes or No	Yes or No	Yes or No	Yes or No	Yes or No	
Player	$10											
Banker	$10											

	Starts with	Did the player roll a sum of 7? CIRCLE ONE										Who won?
		Yes or No	Yes or No	Yes or No	Yes or No	Yes or No	Yes or No	Yes or No	Yes or No	Yes or No	Yes or No	
Player	$10											
Banker	$10											

	Starts with	Did the player roll a sum of 7? CIRCLE ONE										Who won?
		Yes or No	Yes or No	Yes or No	Yes or No	Yes or No	Yes or No	Yes or No	Yes or No	Yes or No	Yes or No	
Player	$10											
Banker	$10											

	Starts with	Did the player roll a sum of 7? CIRCLE ONE										Who won?
		Yes or No	Yes or No	Yes or No	Yes or No	Yes or No	Yes or No	Yes or No	Yes or No	Yes or No	Yes or No	
Player	$10											
Banker	$10											

Is This Game Fair?

Worksheet 1, Page 3

	Starts with	Did the player roll a sum of 7? CIRCLE ONE										Who won?
		Yes or No	Yes or No	Yes or No	Yes or No	Yes or No	Yes or No	Yes or No	Yes or No	Yes or No	Yes or No	
Player	$10											
Banker	$10											

	Starts with	Did the player roll a sum of 7? CIRCLE ONE										Who won?
		Yes or No	Yes or No	Yes or No	Yes or No	Yes or No	Yes or No	Yes or No	Yes or No	Yes or No	Yes or No	
Player	$10											
Banker	$10											

	Starts with	Did the player roll a sum of 7? CIRCLE ONE										Who won?
		Yes or No	Yes or No	Yes or No	Yes or No	Yes or No	Yes or No	Yes or No	Yes or No	Yes or No	Yes or No	
Player	$10											
Banker	$10											

How many times did the banker win? _____

How many times did the player win? _____

Do you think the game is fair after playing these games? Explain your reasoning.

_____

_____

_____

Is This Game Fair?

Class Data Table

Group Number	Number of Times the Banker Won	Number of Times the Player Won
1		
2		
3		
4		
5		
6		
7		
8		
9		
10		
11		
12		
13		
14		
15		
Total		

Now that we have additional data, does it appear that this game is fair?

_____

If you do not think it is fair, how do you think we could change the rules to make it fair?

_____

_____

Is This Game Fair?

Worksheet 2

Name _____

Date _____ Class _____

Written Analysis

What were the results of the games you played? Be as specific as you can in your descriptions.

_____
_____
_____

Did you initially believe the game was fair? Why did you believe that?

_____
_____
_____

Do you still hold that opinion? Why or why not?

_____
_____
_____

After analyzing what happened, what do you think could be done to these rules to make this game more fair?

_____
_____
_____

Work with your partner to design a game using the sum that appears on a pair of dice. Be sure to make the game a fair game. Tell why your game is fair.

_____
_____
_____

DINOSAURS AND PROBABILITY

TEACHER'S PLANNING INFORMATION

Math Topics

Probability, ratio and proportion, data analysis, rounding, estimation

Active Learning

Students will

1. Make a prediction based on their analysis of an experiment

2. Work collaboratively with a classmate to conduct an experiment

3. Use ratio and proportion to problem solve

Materials

Dinosaurs in green, yellow, orange, red, purple, blue (plastic dinosaurs can be purchased in most school supply catalogs. If dinosaurs are not available, a sheet has been provided that can be duplicated on heavy stock in the recommended colors. They can then be cut out for use in the experiment); paper lunch bags; calculators; one Dinosaurs and Probability Worksheet for each pair of students

Suggestions for Instruction

Discuss with the students whether they can predict the colors of the dinosaurs in their bags without looking. They should know the following: (1) There are 12 dinosaurs of varying colors in each bag; (2) they are not to peek in their bags; and (3) after they draw a dinosaur out, they are to tally it on their data collection sheet and then return it to the bag. Ask them to discuss with their partner how many of each color dinosaur they have in their bags and write down their guess. Ask them why you called this a *guess* rather than a *predication*"

The mathematics behind this lesson: Let's suppose that blue dinosaurs were drawn out of the bag eight times and then replaced. Students can set up the following ratio $\frac{8}{36} = \frac{n}{12}$. Using proportions, we can compute that $n = 2\frac{2}{3}$ which rounds to 3. Our prediction would be that there are between two and three blue dinosaurs in the bag—most probably three.

When each group has completed their experiment and made their predictions about how many of each color dinosaur they have in their bags, ask them to be prepared to share their thoughts with the class about why this activity made their prediction more or less accurate than their original guess.

Selected Answers

Answers will vary.

Variation

A similar experiment can be done with students where they can look into the bag and record how many of each color are in the bag. Then conduct the same experiment and see how close their experimental results were to the theoretical.

Writing in Math

Journal questions:

1. Explain how you used ratio and proportion to predict the number of each color of dinosaur in your bag.

2. Suppose there were 25 dinosaurs in your bag. You and your partner draw out and replace a dinosaur 100 times. You draw out an orange dinosaur 13 times. About how many orange dinosaurs do you predict are in the bag? Explain how you solved this problem.

Dinosaurs and Probability

Worksheet: Data Collection

Name _____

Date _____ Class _____

Do you think you can predict how many of each color of dinosaurs there are in a paper bag without looking? This experiment will see if you can do just that.

Directions: Twelve randomly colored dinosaurs have been placed into each paper lunch bag. With your partner, draw one dinosaur from the bag and record its color in the following table. Be sure not to look into the bag. Use tally marks to record each pick, then return the dinosaur to the bag and shake it up. Draw another dinosaur and record the color of the second one. Do this a total of 36 times. Use your results to predict how many of each of the colors is in the bag.

Color	Tally	Ratio $\dfrac{n}{36}$	Proportion $\dfrac{n}{36} = \dfrac{d}{12}$	Decimal	Prediction (Round to the nearest 1)
Green					
Yellow					
Red					
Orange					
Purple					
Blue					
Totals					

Now, count the dinosaurs in your bag.

Were your predictions close? _____

Why do you think you got the results you did? _____

If you are not satisfied with your results, how do you think you could alter the experiment to have more accurate results? Write your answer on the back of this page.

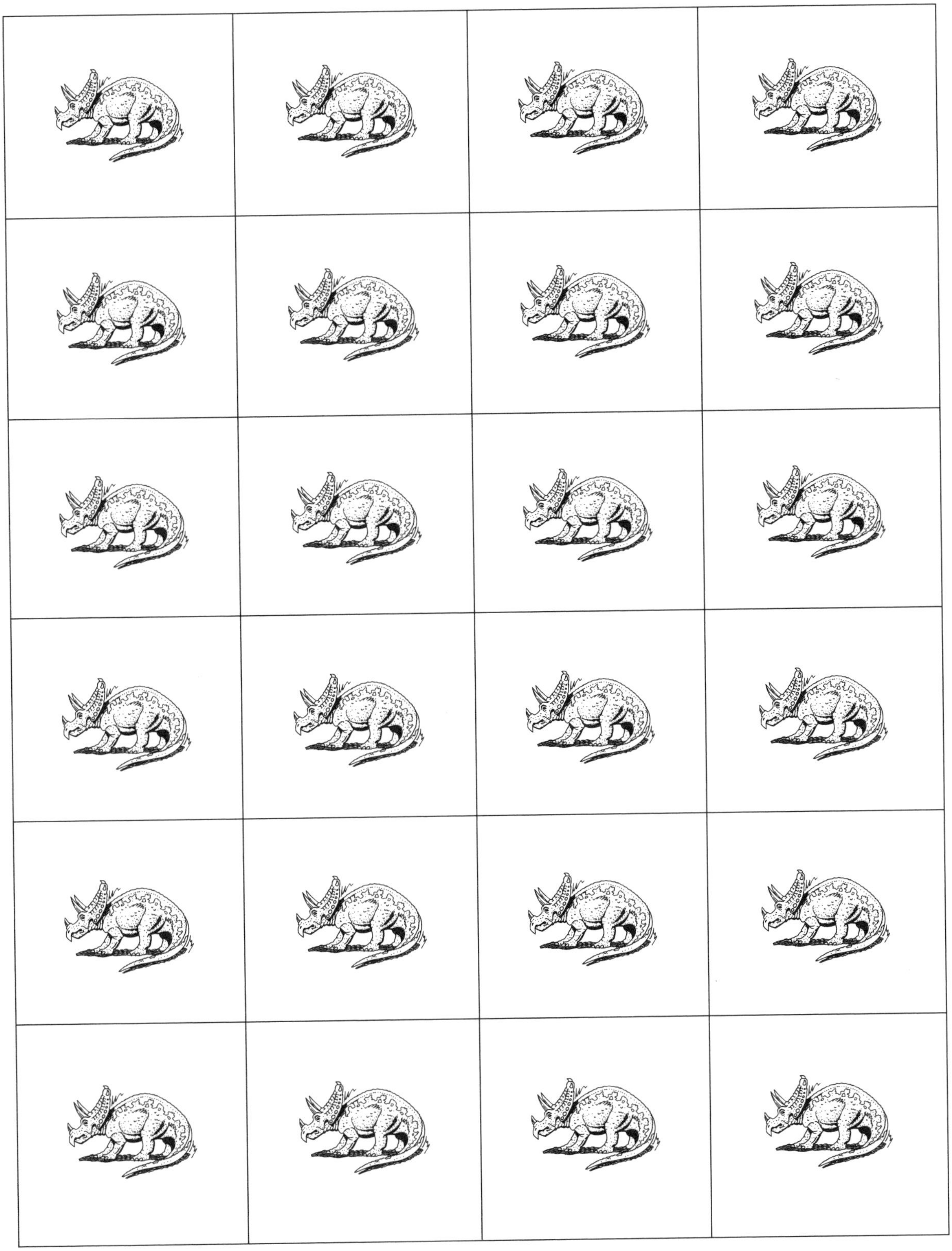

Resource

INTERACTIVE WEB SITES TO MAKE MATH-TECHNOLOGY CONNECTIONS

http://www.shodor.org/interactivate/activities/index.html#fun

This site was referenced in a number of the activities, but it is such a high-quality site that it deserves another mention here. It has interactive activities related to number and operation, geometry and measurement, functions and algebra, and probability and data analysis concepts.

http://www.brunnermath.com/algebraiiiandtrig.htm

This site includes work with prealgebra concepts, such as integers, scientific notation, unit conversion, fractions, and more. When teachers enter this page, they can choose from prealgebra, basic algebra, algebra, algebra 2, or trigonometry problems. The home page offers puzzles, geometry, calculus, and much more.

http://www.pbs.org/teachersource/math.htm

This site is also referenced in some of the activities, but again, it is a very interesting site. The teacher can choose a grade level preference from preschool through high school and then from 10 different mathematics strands. Some very creative investigations are offered.

http://www.cut-the-knot.org/content.shtml

This site is a collection of games, puzzles, and math enrichment topics. It is worth the time needed to explore its wide variety of mathematics oddities.

http://nces.ed.gov/nceskids/graphing/

A very user-friendly site that produces bar, line, area, pie, and coordinate graphs using student data.

http://illuminations.nctm.org/

The NCTM's Web site contains many on-line activities for K–2, 3–5, 6–8, or 9–12 teachers. Once a grade level is chosen, interactive activities are displayed that reflect the content and process standards. There are activities to help students understand a variety of graphic representations, number theory, and much more.

References

Ahmed, A. (1987). *Better mathematics.* London: Her Majesty's Stationery Office.

Chapman-Fahey, M. (1993, November). *Quilt-it bee math?* Paper presented at the National Council of Teachers of Mathematics Regional Conference, Paducah, KY.

Foundation Coalition. (n.d.) *Cone of learning.* Retrieved October 5, 2006, from http://www.foundationcoalition.org

Fuys, D., Geddes, D., & Tischler, R. (1988). *The van Hiele model of thinking in geometry among adolescents in JRME* (monograph number 3). Reston, VA: NCTM.

Lasky, K. (1994). *The librarian who measured the earth.* Boston: Little, Brown Publishers,

Martin, H. (1991). Is this game fair? In J. S. Zawojewski (Ed.), *Dealing with data and chance* (pp. 12–14). Reston, VA: National Council of Teachers of Mathematics.

National Council of Teachers of Mathematics. (1990). *Algebra for everyone.* Reston, VA: Author.

National Council of Teachers of Mathematics. (1999). *Algebraic thinking: Grades 6–12.* Reston, VA: Author.

National Council of Teachers of Mathematics. (2000). *Principles and standards for school mathematics.* Reston, VA: Author.

National Research Council, Mathematical Sciences Education Board. (1989). *Everybody counts: A report to the nation on the future of mathematics education.* Washington, DC: National Academies Press.

Paulos, J. A. (2001). *Innumeracy: Mathematical illiteracy and its consequences.* New York: Hill and Wang.

Sobel, M. A., & Maletsky, E. M. (1998). *Teaching mathematics: A sourcebook of aids, activities, and strategies* (3rd ed.). Boston: Allyn & Bacon.

Stenmark, J. K. (1989). *Assessment alternatives in mathematics.* Berkeley, CA: University of California, EQUALS.

Van de Walle, J. (2006). *Elementary and middle school mathematics: Teaching developmentally* (6th ed.). Boston: Allyn & Bacon.

Willoughby, S. S. (1990). *Mathematics education in a changing world.* Alexandria, VA: Association of Supervisors of Curriculum Development.